Jerome Beker
Douglas Magnuson
Editors

Residential Education as an Option for At-Risk Youth

"**H**aving worked over three decades in Settlement Houses, Child Care institutions, Public School Districts, with Street Gangs and youth at risk in a variety of settings, I believe that the authors have zeroed in on and illuminated the great issue and tragedy of our time–the loss of community, as the "supportive womb" for family and youth, and our ineffective use of it, both as the small "peer group" community and the greater aggregate community-at-large. They show how the community is the collaborative, extended support and therapeutic system, and how it challenges youth to meet social standards–how it is the mirror for youth to look into for self-appraisal and critical self-evaluation–how it is the laboratory for youth to practice and rehearse learned social skills and essential values for effective citizenship–and how to live in a culturally diverse environment–the peer and at-large community is shown as the barometer for youth to continually assess their potential and capabilities.

While the seven (7) models exemplified are not American, the implications have significant meaning for programs in this country, and bode well for consideration for implementation for youth at risk in residential settings.

Many youth at risk have become alienated and many among them are becoming "aliens" in society, in the sense that the distance between their norms and coping abilities, and those of the mainstream, has widened considerably.

The authors present some interesting and useful observations of techniques used by staff to endeavor to bridge the gap, to hold, motivate and ease youth at risk back into the mainstream to a place they deserve and can effectively perform."

Jack A. Kirkland, MA
Associate Professor
George Warren Brown
School of Social Work
Washington University
St. Louis, Missouri

"This is a must-read book for anyone responsible for the development or delivery of residential youth services. The recurring theme offered by the seven inter-related articles offers an optimistic alternative to the negativism and malaise which has gripped residential programming in the U.S.

The authors highlight a common philosophical theme–that the types of youth care services which best serve their target populations are rooted in developmental (identity) education rather than in a treatment framework. Recurring contrasts portray various Israeli and European model of residential care against typical U.S.-driven concepts which highlight notions of control, measurement and efficiency.

Brief descriptions of residential education in Israel stress the positive valuation of youth by administration and staff as well as opportunities for youth choice and access to growth-enhancing experiences. In contrast, the U.S. generally has . . . "Formal organizational structures (which) are typically designed in such a way as to limit growth–to restrict freedom, autonomy, trust and self-awareness."

Lest readers regard such foreign examples as non-translatable to U.S. service system needs, the authors repeatedly remind us that there appears to be a great deal of overlap in the encountered youth populations. With some U.S. exceptions noted, e.g., Job Corps and Neighborhood Youth Corps, the very different national youth care styles emphasize contrasting task conceptions. Cited Israeli and European models primarily involve "learning and building" rather than "rescue or treatment" which is the standard U.S. model. Magnuson, Barnes and Beker conclude, "Organizing a program along pedagogical and human development principles is a necessity."

This book provides stimulating insights for and great challenges to our management-oriented youth services field. Perhaps a follow-up volume will offer more extensive information about the unique humanistic program elements they identify overseas."

Sherwood B. Chorost, PhD, ABPP
Private Practice
formerly Director
of Psychological Services
at Mission of the Immaculate Virgin
& St. Cabrini Home
(two residential treatment programs
in N.Y.)

More pre-publication
REVIEWS, COMMENTARIES, EVALUATIONS . . .

"**I**n *Residential Education as an Option for At-Risk Youth*, Beker and Magnuson have authored a much-needed fresh look at developmentally-oriented residential care for older children, as practiced in Israel and Western Europe, and make a case for its adoption to meet the needs of growing numbers of alienated youths in the United States.

This book presents a fundamental alternative and challenge to the ways we commonly provide residential care today and offers an important and well-tested option for those responsible for finding answers to the problem of growing numbers of youths who lack stable homes and prospects for productive future lives. It should command the serious attention of practitioners and policy makers alike."

George Thomas, PhD
President
Thomas Cottage Industries, Inc.
160 Richard Way
Athens, GA 30605

"**R**eaders will find the penetrating analyses of group care services in Israel, Europe and the United States, together with the implications for policy and practice, timely and insightful. The authors convincingly argue that we can turn the Israeli and European experience to the benefit of our own youth programs if we have the vision and the courage to incorporate the perspicacious insights into our own youth services and leadership endeavors.

Readers do not need be reminded that the United States is facing a crisis in the development and care of its youth, particularly those at-risk. As America flounders in its provisions for the disadvantaged, this book provides intelligent, thought-provoking ideas for more than just dealing with the "bureaucracy and anarchy" in our services to at-risk youth. It provides readers with real help in revising our vision as well as the means for fulfilling it."

A. Harry Passow
The Jacob H Schiff Professor
Emeritus of Education
Teachers College
Columbia University

The Haworth Press, Inc.

Residential Education
as an Option for At-Risk Youth

ALL HAWORTH BOOKS AND JOURNALS
ARE PRINTED ON CERTIFIED
ACID-FREE PAPER

Residential Education as an Option for At-Risk Youth

Jerome Beker
Douglas Magnuson
Editors

The Haworth Press, Inc.
New York · London

Residential Education as an Option for At-Risk Youth has also been published as *Residential Treatment for Children & Youth*, Volume 13, Number 3 1996.

The development, preparation, and publication of this work has been undertaken with great care. However, the publisher, employees, editors, and agents of The Haworth Press and all imprints of The Haworth Press, Inc., including The Haworth Medical Press and Pharmaceutical Products Press, are not responsible for any errors contained herein or for consequences that may ensue from use of materials or information contained in this work. Opinions expressed by the author(s) are not necessarily those of The Haworth Press, Inc.

The Haworth Press, Inc., 10 Alice Street, Binghamton, NY 13904-1580 USA

Library of Congress Cataloging-in-Publication Data

Residential education as an option for at-risk youth / Jerome Beker, Douglas Magnuson, editors.
    p. cm.
    Also published as: Residential treatment for children & youth, v. 13, no. 3, 1996.
    Includes bibliographical references and index.
    ISBN 1-56024-818-1 (alk. paper)
    1. Problem children–Institutional care. 2. Problem youth–Institutional care. I. Beker, Jerome. II. Magnuson, Douglas.
HV862.R473 1996
362.7′4–dc20   96-12415
                                                              CIP

INDEXING & ABSTRACTING

Contributions to this publication are selectively indexed or abstracted in print, electronic, online, or CD-ROM version(s) of the reference tools and information services listed below. This list is current as of the copyright date of this publication. See the end of this section for additional notes.

- *Applied Social Sciences Index & Abstracts (ASSIA) (Online: ASSI via Data-Star) (CD-Rom: ASSIA Plus)*, Bowker-Saur Limited, Maypole House, Maypole Road, East Grinstead, West Sussex RH19 1HH, England

- *Cambridge Scientific Abstracts*, *Health & Safety Science Abstracts*, Environmental Routenet (accessed via INTERNET) 7200 Wisconsin Avenue #601, Bethesda, MD 20814

- *Child Development Abstracts & Bibliography*, University of Kansas, 2 Bailey Hall, Lawrence, KS 66045

- *CNPIEC Reference Guide: Chinese National Directory of Foreign Periodicals*, P.O. Box 88, Beijing, People's Republic of China

- *Criminal Justice Abstracts*, Willow Tree Press, 15 Washington Street, 4th Floor, Newark, NJ 07102

- *Criminology, Penology and Police Science Abstracts*, Kugler Publications, P.O. Box 11188, 1001 GD Amsterdam, The Netherlands

- *Exceptional Child Education Resources (ECER), (online through DIALOG and hard copy)*, The Council for Exceptional Children, 1920 Association Drive, Reston, VA 22091

- *Index to Periodical Articles Related to Law*, University of Texas, 727 East 26th Street, Austin, TX 78705

- *International Bulletin of Bibliography on Education*, Proyecto B.I.B.E./Apartado 52, San Lorenzo del Escorial, Madrid, Spain

(continued)

- *INTERNET ACCESS (& additional networks) Bulletin Board for Libraries ("BUBL"), coverage of information resources on INTERNET, JANET, and other networks.*
  - JANET X.29: UK.AC.BATH.BUBL or 00006012101300
  - TELNET: BUBL.BATH.AC.UK or 138.38.32.45 login 'bubl'
  - Gopher: BUBL.BATH.AC.UK (138.32.32.45). Port 7070
  - World Wide Web: http://www.bubl.bath.ac.uk./BUBL/home.html
  - NISSWAIS: telnetniss.ac.uk (for the NISS gateway)

  The Andersonian Library, Curran Building, 101 St. James Road, Glasgow G4 ONS, Scotland

- *Inventory of Marriage and Family Literature (online and CD/ROM)*, Peters Technology Transfer, 306 East Baltimore Pike, 2nd Floor, Media, PA 19063

- *Mental Health Abstracts (online through DIALOG)*, IFI/Plenum Data Company, 3202 Kirkwood Highway, Wilmington, DE 19808

- *Psychological Abstracts (PsycINFO),* American Psychological Association, P.O. Box 91600, Washington, DC 20090-1600

- *Sage Family Studies Abstracts (SFSA)*, Sage Publications, Inc., 2455 Teller Road, Newbury Park, CA 91320

- *Social Planning/Policy & Development Abstracts (SOPODA)*, Sociological Abstracts, Inc., P.O. Box 22206, San Diego, CA 92192-0206

- *Social Work Abstracts*, National Association of Social Workers, 750 First Street NW, 8th Floor, Washington, DC 20002

- *Sociological Abstracts (SA)*, Sociological Abstracts, Inc., P.O. Box 22206, San Diego, CA 92192-0206

- *Sociology of Education Abstracts,* Carfax Publishing Company, P.O. Box 25, Abingdon, Oxfordshire OX14 3UE, United Kingdom

- *Special Educational Needs Abstracts*, Carfax Information Systems, P.O. Box 25, Abingdon, Oxfordshire OX14 3UE, United Kingdom

- *Violence and Abuse Abstracts: A Review of Current Literature on Interpersonal Violence (VAA)*, Sage Publications, Inc., 2455 Teller Road, Newbury Park, CA 91320

(continued)

SPECIAL BIBLIOGRAPHIC NOTES

related to special journal issues (separates)
and indexing/abstracting

❏ indexing/abstracting services in this list will also cover material in any "separate" that is co-published simultaneously with Haworth's special thematic journal issue or DocuSerial. Indexing/abstracting usually covers material at the article/chapter level.

❏ monographic co-editions are intended for either non-subscribers or libraries which intend to purchase a second copy for their circulating collections.

❏ monographic co-editions are reported to all jobbers/wholesalers/approval plans. The source journal is listed as the "series" to assist the prevention of duplicate purchasing in the same manner utilized for books-in-series.

❏ to facilitate user/access services all indexing/abstracting services are encouraged to utilize the co-indexing entry note indicated at the bottom of the first page of each article/chapter/contribution.

❏ this is intended to assist a library user of any reference tool (whether print, electronic, online, or CD-ROM) to locate the monographic version if the library has purchased this version but not a subscription to the source journal.

❏ individual articles/chapters in any Haworth publication are also available through the Haworth Document Delivery Services (HDDS).

Residential Education as an Option for At-Risk Youth

CONTENTS

ABOUT THE EDITORS

Jerome Beker, EdD, is Professor in the Youth Studies Program of the School of Social Work at the University of Minnesota in St. Paul. He also holds an appointment in the Center for Advanced Studies in Child Welfare and is Adjunct Professor in the Department of Educational Psychology. For over ten years, he directed the University of Minnesota's Center for Youth Development and Research. Previously, Dr. Beker held appointments at Syracuse University, at the State University of New York at Stony Brook, and in several residential group care settings, including the Berkshire Farm for Boys in Canaan, New York, and the Hawthorne Cedar Knolls and Linden Hill Schools in Hawthorne, New York. He is Editor of *Child and Youth Care Forum* and *Child & Youth Services* and the author of several books, including *Critical Incidents in Child Care: A Case Book* and, together with Zvi Eisikovits, edited *Knowledge Utilization in Residential Child and Youth Care Practice.*

Douglas Magnuson, MA, is Research Coordinator for the Project on Vocation, Work, and Youth Development at the College of St. Catherine in St. Paul, Minnesota. In addition, he is a doctoral candidate in Educational Psychology with an emphasis in Social Psychology at the University of Minnesota. His experience includes work in a variety of residential and community settings, including the Creek Valley Teaching Family Group Home in Marquette, Michigan, and two agencies operated by the Salvation Army. He is the author of several articles and, in 1993, co-edited a special issue of *Child and Youth Care Forum.*

Foreword

Residential treatment centers have always steered a course between bureaucracy and anarchy. It's in the nature of the work: the various state bureaucracies that purchase our services must be sure we are safe and non-controversial for their clients, but these same clients have had years of experience fending off our sorts of help; for us to reach them we must be creative, even surprising, in our interactions. Most residential treatment center directors are on the lookout for better, newer, and cheaper programs, and the direct care staff are idealistic and open to new ideas. Perhaps directors more easily accept changes in physical plant and program descriptions than changes in administrative style or direct care staff attitudes, but willy nilly, change is in the air.

All around us we see the old bureaucracies breaking up and the shift of power–internationally, nationally, and in local militias. The states are lagging behind, but soon will be demanding new programs for youth. If we have trouble providing them it will probably be because we have slid into bureaucratic ruts, for example, in squelching surface behavior by point systems, rather than welcoming the "problem" behavior as an opportunity for engagement with the student, however anarchic that engagement may be.

Currently there is much interest in changes in administrative structure, from traditional control based in hierarchies to what is sometimes called Total Quality Management (TQM), as described by authors such as Tom Peters (1992) and Chris Argyris (1993), books such as *Managing the Residential Treatment Center in Troubled Times* (Northrup, 1994), and journals such as *Residential Treatment for Children & Youth* and *Child and Youth Care Forum*. Applied to larger organizations, Total Quality Management implies decentralization, and applied to residential treatment centers, it proposes empowering the direct care staff, giving them more responsibility, initiative, and independent judgement.

Carrying out this sort of organizational change can be tumultuous but in

[Haworth co-indexing entry note]: "Foreword." Northrup, Gordon. Co-published simultaneously in *Residential Treatment for Children & Youth* (The Haworth Press, Inc.) Vol. 13, No. 3, 1996, pp. xv-xvi; and: *Residential Education as an Option for At-Risk Youth* (ed: Jerome Beker and Douglas Magnuson) The Haworth Press, Inc., 1996, pp. xiii-xiv. Single or multiple copies of this article are available from The Haworth Document Delivery Service [1-800-342-9678, 9:00 a.m. - 5:00 p.m. (EST)].

the end is usually inspiring to the staff and helpful to the students. Years ago I was a consultant to the staff of the first special education class in the local public schools. We were filled with the inspiration of a new organization, sure we would overcome local predictions of failure and reach and cure these students, retarded and psychotic alike! We did help them remarkably well, though in retrospect we had only the most general and expedient idea of what we were doing. I suspect something of this inspired energy can be seen in the enthusiastic style of the Total Quality Management authors.

Thus, change is coming, and we can sketch one direction of change toward decentralization, in nation-wide social services, in the states (for example in purchase of services), and locally in the residential treatment centers. Less clear is what these future residential treatment programs should look like in detail, and how to plan for the interactions "where the action is," between the direct care worker and student. Needed are concrete examples of successful programs with samples of the interactions between empowered staff and their hopefully empowered students. It was for this reason that I was enthusiastic about a report from Jerry Beker and Doug Magnuson on seven ongoing successful programs in Israel, and asked them to prepare this group of papers and edit the present volume. The students in these Israeli programs (and in their European counterparts) have problems and needs much like our students, and similar programs could probably be started in the United States for costs comparable to our present program costs, because of the relatively low staff/student ratio.

I hope these papers rouse similar enthusiasm in the reader, and hope some day to publish reports of the establishment of similar programs in the United States.

Gordon Northrup, MD

REFERENCES

Argyris, C. (1993). *Knowledge for action: A guide for overcoming barriers to organizational change.* San Francisco: Jossey-Bass.

Northrup, G., Ed. (1994). *Managing the residential treatment center in troubled times.* Binghamton, NY: The Haworth Press, Inc.

Peters, T. (1992). *Liberation management: Necessary disorganization for the nanosecond nineties.* New York: Alfred A. Knopf, Inc.

Acknowledgements

The editors wish to acknowledge in particular the contributions of Heidi Goldsmith, now Executive Director of the International Center for Residential Education, and Hannah Levin, Director of Israel Affairs of the National Council of Jewish Women, whose shared vision led to the development of the seminar that made this publication possible and whose hard work over many months brought the project to fruition. May their dream that this effort will contribute to the establishment of more humane and effective services for troubled and troubling youth in America be realized! Additional assistance was provided by the Minnesota Agricultural Experiment Station, the School of Social Work, the School's Center for Advanced Studies in Child Welfare (sponsored by the Bush Foundation, the State of Minnesota Department of Human Services, and Title IV-E of the Adoption Assistance and Child Welfare Act of 1980 [Public Law 96272]), and the College of Human Ecology of the University of Minnesota. We are also most appreciative of the unfailing support and encouragement of Gordon Northrup, whose vision as Editor of *Residential Treatment for Children & Youth* led to the development of this publication.

Introduction

The editors of this volume and most of its authors, dissatisfied with the conventional professional "wisdom" in the United States that holds that residential group care programs for children and youth are intrinsically flawed and counterproductive, have been engaged for many years in the identification and conceptualization of more effective models for the delivery of residential services. As the need for such programs increases, given overburdened family foster care resources, growing numbers of "zero-parent" families and homeless youth, and rising demands for youth incarceration, this quest grows as a moral as well as a practical imperative. This volume reports on residential programs in Israel, draws comparisons with their European counterparts, and suggests practical approaches to the enhancement of such programs in the United States.

We in the United States are not "Johnny-come-latelys" in the domain of quality residential group care; we have had some excellent thinkers and have developed some excellent programs in this field (e.g., the work of Fritz Redl; see Morse, 1991). We also helped to initiate and develop such services in Europe in the aftermath of World War Two (Beker & Barnes, 1990). But it is also true that many of our programs have languished in recent decades, and we have a lot of catching up to do! It is the hope of those who have contributed to this collection that it will accelerate and facilitate our progress in that direction.

The first article reports on a 1993 study seminar on "residential education" in Israel, in which the editors of this volume participated together with other American specialists in youth services and related areas. The seminar was motivated by the search for more effective approaches to the need that has been sketched above. Conclusions and implications for the field in the United States are presented, following descriptions of relevant programs and the problems to which they are addressed.

[Haworth co indexing entry note]: "Introduction." Beker, Jerome, and Douglas Magnuson. Co-published simultaneously in *Residential Treatment for Children & Youth* (The Haworth Press, Inc.) Vol. 13, No. 3, 1996, pp. 1-2; and: *Residential Education as an Option for At-Risk Youth* (ed: Jerome Beker and Douglas Magnuson) The Haworth Press, Inc., 1996, pp. 1-2. Single or multiple copies of this article are available from The Haworth Document Delivery Service [1-800-342-9678, 9:00 a.m. - 5:00 p.m. (EST)].

1

One frequently hears concern expressed about the validity of applying experience from one cultural context to another, and attempts to extrapolate directly across cultures may certainly be misleading. Therefore, the next article, by Herb and Liese Barnes, provides a kind of triangulation, comparing European and Israeli approaches and contextualizing them in the American experience. The authors have been closely involved with American residential programs for many years and have been instrumental through the ILEX program in bringing European youthworkers and thinking to the situation here. Implications of the African-American experience for residential education in the United States are then suggested by Richard English, Dean of the School of Social Work at Howard University and a participant in the 1993 seminar in Israel.

Zvi Levy, who directs one of the Israeli programs (Levy, 1993) that is widely recognized as exemplary, provides a conceptual analysis of the approach reflected by that program and by many others in Israel. This is followed by a discussion of the organizational and fiscal practicalities in the context of emerging new approaches to management, authored by Doug Magnuson, Herb Barnes, and Jerry Beker. Heidi Goldsmith, one of the seminar organizers, and Andy Hahn, a Brandeis University specialist in youth policy, then discuss relevant federal policy implications and prospects that might facilitate the dissemination and implementation of more effective models. The volume concludes with a short overview by the editors in which they explore some salient issues and project possible next steps.

It is the editors' hope that this compilation will illuminate not only the possibilities for program enhancement in the United States that are inherent in the models being examined from abroad, but also the practicality of applying such approaches here within current fiscal and other realities, along with the barriers that will need to be overcome.

Jerome Beker
Douglas Magnuson

REFERENCES

Beker, J., & Barnes, F. H. (1990). The educateur returns to America: Approaching the development of child and youth care cross-culturally through ILEX. *Child and Youth Care Quarterly, 19*(3), 161-175.

Levy, Z. (1993). *Negotiating positive identity in a group care community: Reclaiming uprooted youth.* Binghamton, NY: The Haworth Press, Inc. (Also published as *Child & Youth Services*, 1993, *16*(2)).

Morse, W. C. (Ed.). (1991). *Crisis intervention in residential treatment: The clinical interventions of Fritz Redl.* Binghamton, NY: The Haworth Press, Inc. (Also published as *Residential Treatment for Children & Youth*, 1991, *8*(4)).

Residential Education
as an Option for At-Risk Youth:
Learning from the Israeli Experience

Jerome Beker
Douglas Magnuson

SUMMARY. In January 1993, a group of American professionals in the field of child and youth services gathered in Jerusalem for a ten-day seminar designed to enable them to explore Israeli residential group care programs. Their objective was to glean information

---

The authors wish to acknowledge the support of the organizers and sponsors of the seminar–the National Council of Jewish Women, USA (NCJW) in the framework of the U.S.-Israel Memorandum of Understanding, Council of Jewish Federations (MOU)–and the conceptual and programmatic leadership of Hannah Levin and Heidi Goldsmith on behalf of those two organizations, respectively. In Israel, the Seminar was hosted and implemented by the NCJW Research Institute for Innovation in Education at the School of Education of The Hebrew University of Jerusalem and led by Professor Chaim Adler, Professor Elite Olshtain, and Rachelle Schilo. The support provided by the Minnesota Agricultural Experiment Station, the School of Social Work, the School's Center for Advanced Studies in Child Welfare (sponsored by the Bush Foundation, the State of Minnesota Department of Human Services, and Title IV-E of the Adoption Assistance and Child Welfare Act of 1980 [Public Law 96272]), and the College of Human Ecology, University of Minnesota, was also essential and is acknowledged with appreciation.

Address correspondence to the authors: c/o Youth Studies Program, School of Social Work, University of Minnesota, 386 McNeal Hall, 1985 Buford Avenue, St. Paul, MN 55108.

[Haworth co-indexing entry note]: "Residential Education as an Option for At-Risk Youth: Learning from the Israeli Experience." Beker, Jerome, and Douglas Magnuson. Co-published simultaneously in *Residential Treatment for Children & Youth* (The Haworth Press, Inc.) Vol. 13, No. 3, 1996, pp. 3-48; and: *Residential Education as an Option for At-Risk Youth* (ed: Jerome Beker and Douglas Magnuson) The Haworth Press, Inc., 1996, pp. 3-48. Single or multiple copies of this article are available from The Haworth Document Delivery Service [1-800-342-9678, 9:00 a.m. - 5:00 p.m. (EST)].

3

that might be helpful in enhancing services to marginal, disattached youth in the United States. A brief description of the existing need in the U.S. is followed by an overview of the history of such programs in Israel and their underlying conceptualizations. Seven Israeli programs are then described in depth as the basis for the elaboration of 17 philosophical and programmatic themes that emerged from the observations as issues for possible consideration in the U.S. context. *[Article copies available from The Haworth Document Delivery Service: 1-800-342-9678.]*

Despite the conventional "wisdom" in the field that has tended to reject out of hand the exploration of residential group care alternatives in child and youth services, many professionals and academics have continued to support the efficacy of such programs in appropriate situations. Over 25 years ago, for example, Martin Wolins initiated research that sought to define the critical elements of selected Israeli and Eastern European approaches to residential group care for children and youth, which appeared to be more successful than analogous programs in the U.S. His report on this work (Wolins, 1969) has become a classic in the field, supplemented by extended material in his subsequent publications (e.g., Wolins, 1974; Wolins & Gottesmann, 1971).

The subsequent work of Eisikovits and Beker (1986b) focused on Israel and was based on a similar premise, that the Israeli experience in this field could inform and help to enhance such programs in the U.S. Around the same time, Thomas Linton, who had pioneered in bringing Western European approaches to the attention of the field in the United States and Canada (Linton, 1969a, 1969b, 1971), learned about and became interested in the Israeli programs, some of which he visited and studied while on sabbatical in 1988. He returned convinced that therein lay the potential for some kinds of out-of-home services that increasingly appear to be needed in the U.S. and, as a result, he attempted to organize a project designed to expose American professionals in the field to what he had observed in Israel, but he fell victim to cancer before those plans could come to fruition.

Linton's proposals in this connection did, however, help to shape the thinking that, via the involvement of Jerome Beker (who had made similar observations while in Israel on a Fulbright in 1988-89 [Beker, 1990]), led to the development of an intensive study seminar in Israel in 1993. The participants, who were self-selected following a broad search, included 25 U.S. child and youth care professionals–youth policy advocates, university faculty, program administrators, and practitioners. They visited seven Israeli residential programs and met with many of the leading Israeli figures in this field. The National Council of Jewish Women USA (NCJW), working within the framework of the U.S.-Israel Memorandum of Understanding affiliated with the Council of Jewish Federations (MOU)–and thus continuing its long tradition of service to youth development programming–undertook sponsorship of the seminar.[1]

This article reports on the observations made by the group in the course of the seminar and suggests areas for consideration by colleagues who may be interested in program enhancement in the U.S. It is based on the observations of the authors (both of whom participated in the seminar), on the participants' evaluation forms and comments at the closing session, and on informal interviews with them during and after the program.

HISTORICAL BACKGROUND: WHY ISRAEL?

In the U.S. many children who would formerly have been placed in institutions are being referred to family or treatment foster care, which has been viewed as more like a "real family," hence more desirable. That turns out not always to be the case (Levy, 1996, this volume), particularly as growing numbers of those in need of placement and the severity of their problems tax the supply of good foster homes. The advent of in-home, family-based services, as useful as these can be in appropriate cases, has not been able to meet the need, which appears destined to become more acute as the effects of parental AIDS and drug addiction echo through the population.

In 1990, for example, almost 10% of American children lived in households not headed by a parent at all or on the streets (Gross, 1992). We now even have a phrase for such arrangements, "zero-parent families," notes Soukhanov (1992). Increasingly, we are seeing young people in need of care who would fit the classic definition of "orphan" that led to the original development of orphanages, along with ever more severely troubled youth who cannot be managed or nurtured within their own or available foster families. Indeed, we are already hearing calls for a "return to the orphanage" in this connection, although there appears to be recognition that redefined and updated models are needed (e.g., Ladner, 1990).

Israeli practices may be illuminating in this connection because the historical development of their child and youth services has depended heavily on an institutional care component that is highly valued and appreciated in the society, rather than having become stigmatized as is the case in the United States. Thus, as the point has been made by Eisikovits and

1. Details on the American and Israeli participants are provided in the Appendix.

Beker (1986a) in introducing their review of Israeli approaches for an American audience,

> . . . it seems appropriate to examine the "state of the art" in a society, Israel's, that has enshrined group care over the years as a powerfully effective approach not only in alleviating developmental deficits, but also in maximizing the contributions of its most talented young people. (p. vii)

Residential Education in Israel[2]

According to Gottesmann (1991), "Residential education in Israel is deeply rooted in the tradition of the Jewish people in the Diaspora, as well as in the history of its Renaissance" (p. 179). Living in a yeshiva (a Jewish religious boarding school) to study the Talmud has been an accepted practice for centuries, the forerunner of modern institutions with their emphasis on residential group care and educational processes. Even before the establishment of the modern State of Israel in 1948, residential programs for youth were created within kibbutzim (small, largely self-sufficient collective communities that were established by European and other immigrants) and as separate organizations, often with the educational aim of providing training in agricultural practices while reinforcing the nation-building objectives of their founders.

The emphasis was on the broader purposes of the collective rather than on any real or presumed problems of the residents. In the same spirit that marked the development of summer camping programs in the U.S., kibbutzim and youth villages advocated a return to the idealized outdoor, rural, and agricultural setting where youth could transcend the negative influences of urban life–largely, as they saw it, through "collective agricultural labor" (Weiner, 1986, p. 5). This ideological commitment to the value of manual labor is less prominent today, but many Israeli institutions still have work expectations for their residents (Wolins, 1979).

Within the kibbutz, child care reflected an ideological commitment to creating a radically new society, putting into practice Utopian ideas prevalent at that time. Children did not live with their parents but in their own residences, to be raised by the community and to share communal life with their "brothers" and "sisters" of the kibbutz. This reflected a distrust of

---

2. Although the Seminar included some information and a formal presentation about services for the Arab community in Israel, the present article reports on programs that have been developed largely within and serve primarily the Jewish community.

family life (e.g., Wyniken, 1931, as cited in Weiner, 1986, p. 14), but it indicated a community commitment to child-rearing as well. Educational practices were also radical for their time, applying the educational philosophies of Dewey (1916) and other progressive educators, and were grounded in social justice and human rights ideals.

The final major pre-State influence was the Jewish response to the Holocaust and World War II. Youth Aliyah was founded in the 1930s as an "educational, ideological, and rescue" movement for "outcast" youth (Gottesmann, 1991, p. 179). During and after the war, Youth Aliyah represented "escape and survival" (Smilansky, Kashti, & Arieli, 1982, p. 12) for Jewish children from Europe, many of whom came without parents or other relatives. Youth Aliyah remains a strong presence in the delivery of educational and group care services in Israel.

As an indicator of the degree of difference in emphasis from the U.S., 96% of the children in out-of-home care in Israel are in residential programs, according to Gottesmann (1991), and only 4% are in family foster care. These figures may not reflect the situation with regard to the youngest group of children, but the overall tendency is clear. He adds that, "The schools of education in four of Israel's seven universities have residential education and care chairs; in addition there are two educational research institutes, one of which specializes in the subject" (p. 191).

There are about 400 group care institutions in Israel, a country of 4.5 million people. They are supervised by and receive funding from a variety of sources:

> The Ministry of Education and Culture is responsible for the school programme in all types of residential institutions.
>
> The Ministry of Labour and Social Welfare is responsible for the children in care up to the age of 14 years, and for vocational training centres after 16 years of age. . . .
>
> The Ministry of Defence is responsible for a number of pre-military training centres and two residential boarding schools for cadets. The Ministry of Communication has its own technical boarding school. (Gottesmann, 1991, p. 180-181)

Many residential schools also receive financial and other support from voluntary organizations within Israel and abroad.

Since the establishment of the State of Israel in 1948, residential education services have evolved into four types: yeshivas; agricultural schools; youth villages for immigrant and other socially deprived children; and vocational residential schools (Smilansky, Kashti, & Arieli, 1982, p. 13).

More recently, boarding schools that serve gifted young people, especially those from economically disadvantaged populations, have been established.

Many of these institutions were seen as agents of social mobility, allowing new immigrants and disadvantaged students the opportunity to gain access to resources and opportunities that were otherwise not available to them. They have also traditionally been heterogeneous in regards to economic, social, and educational status. In addition, there is a network of more clinically oriented treatment homes for children. According to Mordecai Arieli of Tel Aviv University, however, despite the increased diversification, "only 2100 of the 43,000 youth in care are residents of care or treatment facilities in the U.S. sense of the word."[3]

Arieli explains the key difference between U.S. and Israeli residential institutions serving troubled youth in terms of the distinction between "residential education" (the concept used in the Israeli context) and "residential care" or "residential treatment" as these terms are used in the U.S., noting the following as characteristic of many residential education centers in Israel: Formal schooling occurs on the campus, where the children study within a normative curriculum; students from the community also study at the school located in the residential campus; the process of caregiving is perceived as an educational process; and such programs do not carry a stigma. They provide "a curriculum of education and a program of care."[4]

Today the population of Youth Aliyah is comprised primarily of three groups: Youth whose families are recent immigrants, primarily Ethiopians and Russians; second or third generation children from immigrant families that have not made a successful transition into Israeli life; and a broader spectrum of youth who have had difficulty in some areas of their lives–e.g., trouble with the law, emotional and behavior problems, academic or cognitive deficits, and/or disruptive family life. These categories are similar to those represented by the kinds of young people who, in relatively large numbers, appear to be in need of services in the U.S. as well. Youth Aliyah also serves a smaller group of youth whose parents live abroad.

---

3. Uncited quotations are from presentations that were made during the seminar.

4. There is also a network of "welfare" institutions not directly affiliated with Youth Aliyah that serves mostly younger children. These appear to be more similar to what exists in the U.S., although they have undoubtedly been shaped to some extent by Israeli cultural influences and by the example of Youth Aliyah. A major longitudinal study of children raised in these institutions suggests that institutional upbringing need not detract from healthy development and successful adjustment later in life (Weiner & Weiner, 1990).

SOME EXEMPLARY PROGRAMS

The seven programs described here represent a range of kinds of services for a variety of populations. In order of presentation, two serve socially disadvantaged adolescents, both new immigrants and others; they differ in that one has a religious orientation and the other does not. The next two are designed for adjudicated delinquents, one an institutional setting and the other a community-based group home. The others include one that emphasizes remedial education for young adolescents (junior high school age), one that offers high school education for students identified as gifted but socially disadvantaged and unlikely to receive a quality education in their home communities, and one that serves delinquent and socially maladjusted older youth in the context of an army base (perhaps a model to be compared to the "boot camp" programs being established for such populations in the U. S.)[5]

1. Hadassim

Hadassim has a history similar to those of other Youth Aliyah-affiliated institutions, although Hadassim is sponsored by the Canadian Hadassah-WIZO organization. It was established after World War II for the "absorption and rehabilitation" of children from Europe. Like the others, it has a high school as well as living areas, but the school also serves regular students from the surrounding community as their regional school. Unlike most of the others, Hadassim also serves elementary school age residents who go to school in the community.

The 500 resident students live in dormitories, each of which houses about 40 children and is supervised by a housefather and a housemother. This cohort usually stays together until the young people leave, usually after high school as they enter the Army. There are also about 1000 day students who attend the high school on the grounds.

Most of the residents come to Hadassim because "they are experiencing home and/or school problems due to one or more of three kinds of distress," explains Zvi Levy, the director, "the consequences of recent immigration, a personal crisis of adolescence, or social offenses." He claims that the specific history of the child is not what is important, because those suffering from any of these kinds of problems have two

---

5. The program descriptions are selective and not always parallel, their intent being to highlight elements of the programs and their underlying philosophies that were of particular interest to the group and appear most likely to have implications for practice in the U.S.

crucial things in common: the experience of uprootedness and a lack of opportunity for normal development. According to Levy,

> Acting out is very similar across different types of distress and the intervention is similar for all. We do not specialize in any particular problem; we do know development. In response to distress, Hadassim's primary educational goal is to facilitate the development of a healthy identity, or to rehabilitate an already distorted developmental process.

Levy has framed Hadassim's practice in the language of Eriksonian developmental theory:

> These children come to us because their original environment amplified their problem rather than helping to solve it, so that their problem disrupted their normal developmental process. By treating them as "deviants," their environment helped to aggravate the problem until it became one of deprivation rather than merely deficit. When they come to us the problem is not a didactic one of bridging gaps, but a psychological one of the successful arrangement of a workable configuration of personality fragments.
>
> A positive sense of identity generates an invigorating feeling of a clear destiny rather than a passive sense of fate. Identity formation is the process of organization and reorganization of the individual's qualities and traits and his integration in a clear and relevant surrounding world. Disruption of the healthy process of identity formation leads to identity confusion, a state of anxiety that can paralyze the ability to act.
>
> Identity confusion plays a significant role in behavioral deviations and scholastic failure. Sometimes cumulative disruptions in the developmental process create a "negative identity," a state of mind in which a person feels that his only way of communicating with others or organizing his inner world is by bringing to the fore his weaknesses rather than his strengths. . . . The underlying assumption is that most critical to the development of cohesive identity is the opportunity to experience personal autonomy in a wide range of interpersonal interactions within a flexible educational setting. Reality is tested and grasped through *negotiation* with real people in real situations rather than *rigid laws*. (Levy, 1993a, pp. 3-4)

Youth at Hadassim have almost complete freedom in how they organize their lives, including not only such things as how to decorate their rooms, but also how to spend their time, whether and (within limits) when to go to meals, and which other residents and staff they associate with. By using this freedom of choice, each youth gradually organizes his or her world and, if the climate is supportive, eventually develops and experiences a coherent identity.

Are there really no rules and does this process work? Levy claims that cooperation and obedience eventually arise in the context of the acknowledgement of legitimate authority, rather than through the use of regulations or coercion. There is no formal system of sanctions at Hadassim, and the residents apparently do not lose privileges for misbehavior. As Levy explains it, "The only means (to control behavior) at the staff's disposal is persuasion and negotiation." An exception is made for actual crime, a violation of the law of the land (e.g., drug possession); such offenses are referred for handling by the "experts," the police, with Hadassim serving in what might be viewed as the role of a conscientious parent.

Over the course of several years, a youth at Hadassim has to make 20,000 to 30,000 decisions in this context. Each time, he or she must assess reality, make a judgment about how to act, and accept some responsibility for the consequences. In order for this to produce developmental change, the organization needs to be designed to provide a reality that supports the young person in making such choices and dealing with their consequences, through which a new identity emerges over time.

At Hadassim, they do this in part by not identifying anything other than the most extreme behavior as pathological. This means that there are no psychological labels, no social workers as such, and no formal therapy.[6] In addition, the environment provides opportunities that support identity development and change through relationships with other people–youth and adults–in the living unit, in school, in leisure time activities, etc. These people provide readily available new interpersonal connections for the youth, as well as "models of identification." There is freedom to explore a wide range of planned and spontaneous opportunities for activity and relationship in the context of a strong, easy-to-read culture with a dominant ethical value or "overarching ideology" (Beker & Feuerstein, 1991a, p. 33; Wolins, 1969). "Don't tell a child what to do," says Levy, "tell him who he is."

Hadassim is also organized so as to provide clear feedback to the young people about the impact of what they do. Levy uses the idea of the "no door" policy to demonstrate what this means. Any resident can approach any adult at any time. However, because there are (figuratively) "no

---

6. When needed, such services are provided by appropriate agencies outside the village.

doors," the youth has to assess reality to determine if it is an appropriate time and place. Residents who approach Levy's office must assess and decide whether what they want to talk about is important enough to interrupt what he is doing. They know that they are welcome, but they do not necessarily know if now is the right time. If one decides correctly, he or she is welcomed into the office. One who chooses incorrectly, on the other hand, is not allowed to enter then. Instead of limited "office hours" or universal accessibility, this system requires the child to "assess reality." Learning about the appropriateness of the timing in the context of the particular issue involved and his or her relationship with Levy (or another staff member) helps to shape the child's judgment.

As the youth learns to navigate this new world, he or she gains recognition from the community, recognition that affirms one's new status, role, and identity. This recognition is in sharp distinction to the more conventional use of rewards or reinforcement. It is the result of the young people's fulfillment of their responsibilities in relationship to the community and successful negotiation of a place for themselves, their identity. As Levy says, "It is a recognition of how the youth has changed the (his or her) world."

For example, one who wants to learn to operate the sound equipment in the auditorium must approach the resident responsible for that area, find a way to "hang around," and find an opportunity to contribute. Over the course of time, he or she gains recognition from the community because of its dependence on his or her skills. Every youth at Hadassim has "tentative access" to everything and everybody, meaning that it is the resident's choice of what activities to participate in and with whom to seek relationships.

The emphasis here is on community and permanence of commitment. Residents usually stay until they leave for the army, and they are welcome to return during their army service and afterwards. Some who remove themselves from the program by refusing to be enrolled in school (as opposed to failure to attend on a given day), for example, are permitted to live on the grounds in an unofficial, semi-resident status.

Symbols are viewed as important. According to Levy, the grounds are designed so that the children are at the center of the "universe." The business of Hadassim is conducted openly so that children see how adults live and work. There are no signs on the property, so that visitors have to rely on children to direct them to the appropriate buildings. Levy goes to the dormitories every morning around 6:30 to demonstrate that even the administrators get up early, not just the youth and direct care staff.

As always, questions can be raised about the program. How much of its success can be attributed to the charisma of the director? Does the degree of freedom provided even to upper elementary school age children and the low staff-child ratio leave them a little rambunctious and "too eager" for attention, perhaps feeling starved for affection?

For what types of youth might this kind of environment not be appropriate? Levy claims that Hadassim accepts some of the most troubled children, although he indicates that the program "is not suitable for the adolescent whose developmental process was disturbed at a very early stage of ego development" (Levy, 1993b, p. 119). Hadassim accepts sexual offenders, and there has apparently been little abuse of the freedom that youth have in that connection. There is no subculture of violence, according to Levy, although there are, of course, the kinds of occasional outbursts of anger and conflict that normally occur when young people–or adults, for that matter–live closely together, whether in families or in other congregate living arrangements.

In conclusion, it was apparent that a high degree of affection, physical and otherwise, exists between staff and students. The children at Hadassim present themselves as stunningly happy in comparison to those living in analogous institutions elsewhere. Most cite the freedom they have and their relationships with staff members as key reasons why they like it there. It appears that they do not abuse their freedom–children do go to school, they go to study halls voluntarily, they do take care of one another. As one girl said, "It is beautiful what they do to us here."

2. Yemin Orde–Wingate Children's Village

The visitor to Yemin Orde is first impressed with the physical appearance of the setting: The village sits on the ridge of a mountain, along a road that passes an artist's colony, and overlooks the Mediterranean Sea south of Haifa. The grounds are impeccably maintained and the landscaping is beautiful.

The dining hall is clean and well maintained, with artwork (including students' art) lining the walls and music accompanying the meals. According to the Director, Dr. Chaim Peri, these items are there for educational reasons: The art to acquaint students with masterpieces and with the beauty of their own cultures of origin (many come from Ethiopian, Russian, and other immigrant families); the music for similar reasons, and to get students humming classical, ethnic, and Jewish melodies, which can later be used for instruction. The facilities are designed to arouse a cultural and aesthetic sense and pride in their care and condition. Music, art, and other cultural activities are maintained to provide aesthetic experiences. As Peri puts it, "Beautiful people come from beautiful places."

According to him, everything–from the design and arrangement of the buildings to the way food is served–is done for a reason. The map of Africa hanging on the wall indicates to students that Africa is important. The design of the chapel simulates a tent, symbolizing the Jews wandering in the wilderness as well as having contemporary experiential significance to those residents who have recently arrived from Ethiopia.

The physical separation of the school and living environments on the grounds is part of the ideology–it stands for going from home to school, as one does in a regular community, and creating a productive tension between them, according to Peri. "The school is doomed to be school," he says, meaning that the structure and functions of the school, reflecting the more objective standards and demands of the "real world," dictate that it be a relatively "closed" setting, although attuned to individual needs and differences.

In the community part of the program, however, residents are freer to negotiate their status and their relationships with other people. For example, there are regular votes on the policies of the organization. For education, fun, and serious discussion, residents frequently debate controversial issues. But Peri is clear that Yemin Orde is not a democracy–it is important that residents not have control. "It is open, but structured."

Peri was also relatively uninterested in rules, but there are expectations. Residents can leave the grounds if they want to, for example (some of them help in an Ethiopian immigrant absorption center in Haifa), but they cannot leave after 2:00 p.m. because Yemin Orde does not want its students to be out at night. Students can "run away," but they are required to tell someone where they are going! As Peri puts it to them: "You cannot do that to me [without telling me where you are going]. I have to sleep at night." The orientation is towards the pain that the runaway puts other people through, not on breaking a rule about leaving.

Each residence cottage has a theme that represents a different century. One ring of cottages represents Jewish history, the other, world history. For example, Aristotle Cottage represents the Greek period, Marcus Aurelius represents the Romans, and so on up to Martin Luther King Cottage, representing the 20th Century. Each year the students move "up" from one cottage to another so that even their living arrangements are educational.

Although vocational and academic training are part of the program, the primary orientation of this milieu is towards the restorative effects of community life. Thirty staff families live on site, and many staff members are graduates of the program. "They convey that this is not just another station in life; it has a commitment," says Peri. This commitment apparently replaces the professional distance or boundaries that often separate staff and administrators from residents in residential settings in the United States, as is illustrated by Peri himself:

> Every child that comes here I take to my house, and I show them my bedroom. We want to show them that in every way it is possible to penetrate as deep as you can in my private life. If I let them penetrate into my life, then it helps me with discussion of their family life.

Symbolic communication of this kind is viewed as important. Similarly, the gymnasium was designed so that it would be one of the nicest in the area, with many bleacher seats available, making it possible to hold many of the surrounding community's athletic events there. This is viewed as communicating to the residents that Yemin Orde is a special place that functions within and contributes to mainstream society. Residents produce a television program every day that documents some of the major events on the campus and is viewed in the living cottages, an example of a skill- and esteem-building activity that also serves and strengthens the Yemin Orde community as a whole.

When youth are admitted to Yemin Orde, according to Peri, it makes a permanent commitment to them. This does not last only until the completion of high school, which would be remarkable enough in comparison to the bureaucratically and/or judicially determined limitations that often govern such placements in the United States, but continues throughout life. Yemin Orde performs weddings and conducts marriage counseling for its graduates, co-signs their mortgages when necessary, and provides a transitional home between major life events, like the period between leaving the Army and going to work or school. "It's not our work, it's a life for us here" and it is a (primary or secondary) *home* for the youth. According to Peri, alienation does not long survive in this atmosphere, although not every child might agree with this at every moment.

Recent immigrants from Ethiopia comprise a large proportion of the residents, so the program seeks to adapt to vast cultural differences as it makes work with Ethiopians one of its specialties. Particular care was taken in bringing Ethiopians together with Russian immigrants, who are also well represented in the Yemin Orde population. Since many Russians have been conditioned to be condescending towards Africans, Yemin Orde representatives went to Russia to prepare future residents for the cultural shock of living with black-skinned people. In the same way, representatives, including Peri, went to Ethiopia to learn about their culture (Peri has also learned their language) and to prepare the future immigrants for what they would encounter.

According to Peri, the loyalty of the Ethiopians has been transferred from the tribe to Yemin Orde because they have been supported in their traditions rather than forced to deny them, an observation that may be instructive for others seeking to serve new and different population groups. As the Ethiopians have been encouraged to tell their stories and to share their traditions, he indicated, the general level of understanding of Jewish traditions has been enriched, maybe even corrected, since the new-comers bring practices that more directly reflect ancient Jewish values and beliefs.

Of course, the Ethiopians historically looked forward to the time when they would go to Zion, to Israel, so they tend to be highly motivated to succeed there. Unlike the other settings described, Yemin Orde is a religiously observant community; it supports, reflects in its program, and encourages "Modern Orthodox" practices but does not impose them on individuals. The Yemin Orde students are 13 to 19 years of age, and most are there for reasons directly or indirectly connected to their relatively recent immigration—unaccompanied minors, family disorganization, family poverty, etc.

3. MANOF

Opened in 1975, MANOF has a relatively short history compared to that of most of the other institutions. The program was developed largely by Chaim Adler, who was then Director of the NCJW Research Institute for Innovation in Education at The Hebrew University of Jerusalem, in response to dissatisfaction with what was being done in Israel for youth who dropped out of school and were "disattached" and delinquent. Originally for boys only but now coeducational, MANOF serves slightly over 100 15- to 17-year-olds of "normal" ability and motivation. It has been directed by Yaakov Ohayon since its inception as:

> . . . a place to provide a second chance, in an open, participatory environment, to youngsters who had failed . . . a place where for the first time in their lives they find adults they can trust. It takes in young people who would otherwise be in therapeutic communities and treats them educationally.

Youth come to MANOF voluntarily, so court-ordered placements are not accepted except by mutual agreement among all concerned, including the prospective resident. (Some may, of course, choose to come because of the relative unattractiveness of available alternatives.) The educational philosophy is guided by the principles of personal responsibility, permissiveness, and negotiation. Responsibility for one's behavior and for success in the program is in the hands of each of the youths involved. Consequently, MANOF provides opportunities for success–a place where resources to help youth gain skills are available and where there is an atmosphere that rewards commitment to positive ideals. A conscious attempt is made to focus on excellence and to provide the residents with the best possible educational and group living program.

Responsibility is closely coupled with permissiveness. If the young people are to be responsible for themselves, according to the philosophy of the program, the environment must give them permission to do what they choose to do. This is apparently not the romantic kind of permissiveness of A. S. Neill (1960), not a synonym for freedom or license in the Summerhill sense, for approval of "deviant" behavior, or for a belief in moral relativism. It is, rather, a kind of political liberty, connected to the right of individuals to make basic choices about how they live their lives, coupled with the need to accept responsibility for the consequences. Such an approach might face a difficult challenge from the bureaucratic and legal climate in other jurisdictions, which may hold the institution responsible for youth behavior and require documentation of every event.

There are no therapists or therapy-type practices, in the formal sense, at MANOF. It was stated that "Some youth need only therapy, but they do not come here." As at Hadassim and probably elsewhere, when such services are required by MANOF youth in particular circumstances, they are usually provided in the outside community. There are MANOF clinicians involved in intake decisions, coordination with families, and follow-up, however, and there seems to be some feeling at least in that department that additional clinical services could be helpful.

There is no formal system of sanctions at MANOF. The response to misbehavior and mistakes is to "talk" to the youth; if talking doesn't work, staff members report, they talk again. And if a second talk doesn't work? Again, the staff said, "We talk. We talk and we talk and we talk . . . " According to Adler, they "deny all failures," meaning that they deny that failure has a permanent grip on a youth. No privileges are withheld in response to misbehavior or otherwise, and they do not allow students to blame others for their own problems.

Yet in extreme cases, a youth may be asked to leave the program. As at Hadassim and Yemin Orde, however, there is a near-permanent commitment to the youth, and one can come back as many as ten times. (It was not clear whether "ten times" was a policy or a symbol for infinity.)

Staff members at MANOF believe that adolescence is the right time for dramatic change. By making a voluntary choice to live at MANOF and committing to its ideals, the youth is making the first step toward joining society. Voluntary choices are seen as vital and the program makes the assumption that the needed motivation exists.

MANOF provided the strongest evidence that physical affection between residents and staff has a completely different meaning than in the U.S. Staff members are frequently seen holding hands with, hugging, or caressing students. The director was observed openly running his hands through the hair of a female student, something that would be viewed with concern and even suspicion in the U.S.

The educational program includes both academic and vocational content. Seminar participants noted that males and females were placed in different vocational tracks, with females frequently pointed, for example, toward clerical skills and males toward more mechanical, technical trades. The program day is traditional, with students in school from 8:00 to 1:30, and "enrichment activities" are provided after that. Training is also available in what are called "personal development activities," such as sex education or alcohol counseling. Scheduled time, during which adults are present to supervise and assist, is provided for doing homework.

MANOF started as a one-year program on the grounds of the institution, followed by a year of living with a host family on a kibbutz and/or in a higher education preparatory program at Haifa University, where the group lived as a cohort with staff support. Due to economic and other factors, students now spend two years at MANOF, but the opportunity for college preparation and to go on to the University continues. At the beginning of the program, they take tests of academic or intellectual potential, languages, and mathematics, and they participate in preparatory camp programs. Each youth also spends a day at MANOF before deciding whether to enter the program.

The overall level of student satisfaction with MANOF and commitment to the goals of the program seem high. For example, when one student was asked what he liked about MANOF, his response was, "The atmosphere, a room, a bed, food, a friend, a profession." (Israelis often refer to what Americans might call a trade or a vocation as a profession, due to ambiguities in translation from the Hebrew.)

The core staff members have been at MANOF for several years (the director, since its inception), providing stability to the mission and the program. Direct care staff turnover is about 30% per year. About a quarter of the students leave before completing the program. Such departures tend to be concentrated during the first year, and in two time periods—one early in the year and one late in the year, when residents realize they cannot sustain the effort. As in most of the programs, success is defined largely in terms of the ability of the youth to gain entrance to and to succeed in the military.

4. *ELEM Community Hostel, Tiberias*

ELEM reflects a philosophical framework and history notably different from those of the other programs described, and more similar to the U.S. experience. Lester Zaruches, the director, refers to it as a residential treatment center. It is located within a Tiberias residential neighborhood and appears to operate as what many Americans would call a group home, with between 10 and 20 residents. The youth use the regular, community-based social, educational, recreational, and medical treatment resources available to all residents in the area. ELEM prefers to admit people from nearby rather than from distant communities. In the words of Zaruches, "The children are taught to live in the community while living in a treatment center," and "We teach kids to live in a house, not an institution." The house has no name so that it is not thus distinguished from other homes in the neighborhood.

The youth in residence are 14 to 18 years of age; some have been placed by court order and others are there voluntarily. Most have "dysfunctional families" and need a "family intervention program." Residents stay from one to two and one-half years, hopefully returning home after treatment. They receive individual therapy and group therapy, and there is some form of "family involvement."

Life is maintained according to normal household practices and rules. A youth who breaks a rule may lose privileges to go downtown, to watch TV, or to participate in other activities. All the residents are required to work or go to school; an attempt is made to bring them all at least to the level of a tenth-grade education. Criteria for success are framed as long range goals, like making it into the army. As in other institutions, that is a major motivator, and the hostel faces a challenge in this regard because entrance requirements for the army are becoming more stringent and many hostel graduates are being rejected. Shorter-term goals are based on individual needs, presumably those things that make it possible for the youth to return home.

The organization's philosophy of behavior change appears to be eclectic–a mixture of positive reinforcement, talk, therapy, rewards like pocket money, family counseling, environmental manipulation, etc.–not unlike that of some residential treatment centers in the U.S. However, the emphasis on respecting and on caring for the youth that is noted in the descriptions of the other programs was evident here as well.

The facility itself is a large, attractive house with the usual assortment of common living areas, sleeping areas, and offices. One office has a one-way mirror for observation of therapy sessions. The staffing arrangements for the young people in the program include a housemother who "organizes the culture of the house." Four counselors are there from 4:00 to 8:00 p.m. At other times, the hostel is staffed according to a typical U.S. youth care worker shift system. Funding for the program comes from ELEM, which is a private organization, and from the government.

In language (as translated), culture, and population, the hostel seems typical of a U.S. group home. The use of terms like "counselor," "dysfunctional," "treatment," and "therapy" and the types of treatment arrangements would be very familiar to U.S. practitioners. It is unclear to what extent this may reflect the fact that the director of this particular hostel, Zaruches, is an American who emigrated to Israel a number of years ago, but ELEM sponsors several such hostels throughout the country, and its ideology and approach would be familiar to Americans in any event. Yochanan Wozner, one of the founders, writes that,

> The beginnings of ELEM symbolized the summit of naivete, namely that a few Americans and Israelis can influence the Israeli youth-care system. With fewer than 25 people, less than $2000, off we went to change the system . . . to set up community hostels instead of closed and/or maximum security facilities for juvenile delinquents . . . to include the families instead of taking their children away from them and then "fight their bad influence" . . . to raise the awareness of the community that these kids belong to the community, instead of allowing them to be put away and forgotten . . . to demonstrate that modern educational technology, such as computers, is applicable to youth in distress as well as to the more adjusted . . . to bring the "deviates" together with the "normals" as much as possible. (ELEM, 1992)

5. Kiryat Ye'arim

Kiryat Ye'arim is a two-year residential "preparatory" program for young people of junior high school age and is located in the hills northwest of Jerusalem. It is preparatory in the sense that its purpose is to rehabilitate, within that period, severely socially disadvantaged young people who have failed educationally in the regular schools. Heavy emphasis is placed on the school program, which is based on Reuven Feuerstein's principles of "Instrumental Enrichment" (Feuerstein, Rand, Hoffman, & Miller, 1980) and "Mediated Learning Experience" (Feuerstein, Klein, & Tannenbaum, 1991). The goal is to enable the students, after the two years at Kiryat

Ye'arim, to succeed in the mainstream schools in their home communities or, if home conditions preclude that, in a youth village such as Hadassim or Yemin Orde.

Traditionally, placement in Israeli youth villages was designed to be permanent, in concept if not always in fact, until at least ages 17 or 18. In the late 1950s and 1960s, Youth Aliyah began to experiment with shorter interventions, and in the case of Kiryat Ye'arim focused on cognitive deficits that are at the root of academic problems and, Feuerstein believes, the source of many behavioral and emotional problems as well. The two years (originally one year) are perceived by the youth as well as by the program as a limited time period–a kind of "last chance"–during which they have the opportunity to work on specific, focused goals, and the program now enjoys wide support. (In fact, many youth may have multiple "last chance" opportunities of this kind.) Thus, Kiryat Ye'arim takes students who are rejected by other systems because of their academic and/or behavioral deficiencies. As Feuerstein says, "These are students who have lost the ability to become educated [in a regular school]."

There are four scholastic groupings or tracks based on academic ability. Student time is very structured and the academic curriculum is specific and progresses along a hierarchy of tasks. These children, like the older youth in other residential education settings, are assumed to be motivated by their desire to get into the army. The children also know that at the end of two years they will have more choices about where they go if they work hard now.

There seems to be no sense of a motivation "problem," no belief that motivation is something that needs to be provided from outside or structured into the program. Apparently, the program functions on the basis of a conviction that it is possible for an 11-year-old with behavioral and/or cognitive difficulties to be self-disciplined enough, and to have enough ability to delay gratification, to base his or her study habits on a desire for something that lies two to five years in the future. It should be noted, however, that Feuerstein's Instrumental Enrichment processes present the child with very concrete, practical, intriguing, and enjoyable problems that can become self-motivating.

In one classroom, for example, students might be learning about directions (north, south, east, west, and points between). They start with the basic four directions in reference to a fixed point on the blackboard, working from there to coordinates among the four, then learn to apply directions to a mobile reference point, and then apply these concepts in reference to their own position in relationship to other objects around the classroom and the school. What is crucial, however, is the Instrumental

Enrichment principle of learning to generalize to other situations. In this case, the instructor can expand the idea that directions have meaning only in relationship to something else–relativity–to show how it applies to mathematics, for example, through such concepts as "larger" or "smaller" and "less than" or "more than," which also have meaning only in relation to a point of comparison.

The school environment seeks to adapt itself to the needs of the child, not the other way around. This tells the children that they are important right now, not just as future employees, future soldiers, or future citizens. Instruction starts with the assumption that all the children can learn. A teacher-student ratio of one to two is common at the beginning of a student's stay and eventually becomes one to about 15. The curriculum often begins with games and works up to more complex problems. Students are expected to work about 15 hours per week in addition to their schooling and may have only about an hour per day of free time. According to staff members, the greatest challenge is finding an outlet for each of the children to succeed at something.

Kiryat Ye'arim has a computer resource room, for example, in which students do word processing, art, and various problems on computers. The instructor in charge of this room believes that computers are useful in work with this population because the opportunity to work with exotic equipment is motivating in itself and has the added benefit of reducing the intimidation factor of technology. Computers allow the student to make mistakes and correct them without any intervention by another person, which they might find shaming or judgmental. Finally, computers present opportunities to overcome concrete problems of negotiating the software, which gives students confidence as they become more proficient.

According to the staff, about 5% of the students do not make it through the program. What happens to those who fail to do so is unclear, but the alternative work and/or training options do not appear to be viewed as desirable. About one third or more go home after completing the program, and the rest move on to other residential settings. Where they go is determined largely by their academic progress. There appears to be no stigma associated with having been a student at Kiryat Ye'arim. This is consistent with the historical acceptance in Israel of the desirability of residential education. It does not appear to be consistent with the experiences of many U.S. programs targeted towards children with deficits, which find that their students and programs are generally stigmatized by outsiders.

With regard to disciplinary procedures, the staff reports that, "When they come here they cooperate better because they don't need to act out," implying that misbehavior has a "logic" or rationality for which the educational and social environment of Kiryat Ye'arim does not provide support. This response also suggests the absence of any underlying expectation that these children are likely to act out. Again, there is an assumption of motivation and also of students' responsibility for themselves. For students who are having an immediate problem, the school has what are referred to as "runaway corners" (like the art room or other resource rooms), where students can go by choice at any time. If a student wants to leave the classroom, that is accepted, with the teacher assuming that the student knows what is best for him or herself at that particular moment.

With regard to the staff's expectations for the students, there is no code of rules for students to follow; the only stated requirement is that they finish the program in two years, which they are motivated to do so that they can go on in their education. Yet observation suggests that there are informal behavioral expectations for the students, and that they do not always meet them. After an episode of rambunctious behavior (including a good-natured outburst of excitement centered around a young, tall African-American visitor, who the students decided was a famous American professional basketball player) had delayed classes for some time, for example, some of the teachers were visibly upset and began to shout at the children in an effort to settle things down.

Funding for the program comes from a combination of public and private sources, including a Swiss group that sponsors the program as well as Youth Aliyah and the Israel Ministry of Education. Most of the 180 male and female youth are from lower socioeconomic levels; thus, the population is relatively homogeneous. This departure from the traditional Youth Aliyah ideology (which favors heterogeneous grouping) is a consequence of a deliberate choice to establish an intervention program to meet the needs of a specific disadvantaged group.

6. Armoured Corps Army Base, Ashkelon

The entrance to the army base looked more like what one might associate with that of a summer camp, reflecting the seemingly relaxed and open atmosphere inside. It is not primarily a combat-oriented base; rather, it is responsible for maintenance of army equipment—tanks, trucks, transport vehicles, and the like, as well as a variety of electronic devices. Most of the work is performed at the base, although the maintenance workers follow the combat to provide on-site support in time of war.

There are five main categories of soldiers (male and female) and programs at the Ashkelon base:

1. Regular soldiers serving full time (ages 19-24), who are drafted from the general population of the country, usually shortly after high school, and are the primary source of military personnel.
2. Regular soldiers serving part-time, having finished their two years (for women) or three years (for men) of full-time service and are in school or employed elsewhere but continue to provide periodic military service on a reserve basis.
3. Career soldiers. These are a relatively small proportion of the total number of soldiers, and most are officers.
4. "Underprivileged" soldiers, who are so categorized for a variety of reasons such as academic problems and failure to pass preliminary tests, and who participate in a remedial program. They spend three days of each week doing army work and three days in appropriate educational courses.
5. High school youth, aged 14 and up. This is a pre-service remedial program, ideally making it possible for the participants, who might otherwise be rejected, to join the regular army at a later date.

Placement of regular army inductees is based on nationwide testing and the consequent referral of individuals to specific programs based on their strengths and weaknesses. Those in categories four and five, "marginal" or "underprivileged" soldiers, receive training and mentoring from regular soldiers. After going through the program, those who succeed become "real" soldiers, the idea being that they will receive remedial help at the same time as they are being "mainstreamed." In the process they receive vocational and other training. This Army base is an ideal place to conduct these activities, since the resources allow training in mechanics, electronics, operation and maintenance of heavy equipment, and the like. There are also special programs for inductees who are recent immigrants from Ethiopia.

The basic program format for the disadvantaged soldiers (Group 4) begins with ten days of "absorption" at a base in the north. This is a relatively unstructured period of transition during which the youth and staff spend a lot of time talking together about life in the army. The commanders are taught to be patient. The army has found that this absorption period helps them to resolve problems before they can fester into something worse.

During their tour of duty, these soldiers also receive training in reading and writing Hebrew and in Israeli heritage, and they perform community service, which is felt to intervene in and counter the effects of the participants' earlier pattern of failure and feelings of marginality. There are also substance abuse and family life/sex education components. The curriculum is designed by professionals within the army. The program for the high school youth (Group 5) includes a school program on the grounds together with paramilitary training and many of the same additional components as are provided to the disadvantaged soldiers.

The base commander suggests that there two main reasons for the success of the program. First, the participants are motivated by their desire to be in the army. Even the so-called "underprivileged" or "socially deprived" are so motivated. Second, he claimed that the youth are treated with care and respect. These considerations appear to contrast significantly with stereotypical military practices and culture in the U.S.

With regard to the first point, it should be noted that almost every citizen of Israel–male and female–has traditionally been required to serve in the military, although some are rejected for military service because of academic or cognitive problems, disabilities, or a criminal record. Thus, army service has come to be viewed as the norm and is widely considered to be desirable; the absence of military service carries a stigma that may affect future educational and career prospects as well as social status.

As in the U.S., the military operates as a vehicle of social mobility for those in lower socioeconomic classes. Presumably it does so to a greater degree in Israel because of the draft, which allows few social-class-based exceptions to participation, and because so many Israeli soldiers come from families that have relatively recently immigrated to the country. It also seems to provide and/or reflect a widely shared set of ideological principles, including a core commitment to the defense of Israel and to its national ideals.

In the U.S., although voluntary enlistments have succeeded in meeting its manpower needs in recent years, military service is less broadly viewed as highly desirable by "underprivileged" youth, especially those with family or behavioral problems, or by elite youth, who generally prefer higher education. In addition, care and respect are not values that are usually associated with military programs, including the "boot camp" type programs for youth in trouble that have recently become popular. Sometimes referred to as "shock incarceration," they use hazing, humiliation, and seeming brutality to break down the participants' defenses and indoctrinate them with a new set of norms (Polsky & Fast, 1993, and associated editorial, comments, and rejoinder).[7]

---

7. These programs might be viewed as an institutional manifestation of the "tough love" philosophy. Non-boot-camp programs based on military principles and often using current or former military personnel have begun to emerge as well; the extent to which these reflect principles similar to those of the Israeli programs is unclear.

There also appear to be basic philosophical and psychological differences between the two countries in the dominant understanding of the nature of disadvantage and deprivation and how to change it. At the Israeli army base, one of the staff members notes, "We tell all of the 18-year-olds that they can change," implying that the process of change is one of voluntary choice. Change is also seen as a function of the human values of "care and respect."

These principles appear in marked contrast to U.S. stereotypes of the military. Again, for example, in the boot camp model, change is the result of coercion and control of the subjects' every movement and choice; this may be more extreme than but not totally different from the dominant perspective in some mainstream U.S. residential programs. By contrast, the Israeli military programs for marginal youth appear to be more analogous to those of a progressive youth agency.

The civilian overtones of the army base personnel also seem to be significant: They appeared to be people with a variety of nonmilitary interests serving in military roles and settings. Several have degrees in non-military fields, including the head of the program for disadvantaged soldiers on the base, a woman who was working on a doctorate in anthropology. It is also noteworthy that the Israeli military is much more closely connected to daily civilian life, since soldiers are permitted to go home frequently (some every weekend) and distances are short in such a small country. Seeing soldiers hitchhiking along the road or riding buses with civilians is routine. All of these factors may help to "normalize" the experience of the young people for whom the army functions as a socially and educationally remedial tool.

7. Boyar High School

Boyar is an elite residential school in Jerusalem serving capable but disadvantaged 7th through 12th graders from "development towns" around the country together with academically gifted day students from the Jerusalem area. The total student population is about 800. Although its elite status differentiates it from most other Israeli residential education programs, the goal of the educational process is similar: "The social integration of the next generation in Israeli society."

Boyar draws most of its students from lower socioeconomic class families and seeks to give them a top quality education, with the hope that it will expand their opportunities for social mobility as well as enable them to make a contribution to the country. They are selected from nominations by their teachers and principals based on an annual solicitation. The staff does not believe that the program represents elitism in the negative sense of that term; in fact, they say, by giving poor students the best education possible and preparing them for leadership roles, they are providing "justice to the needy in society."

The Boyar staff also emphasizes a theme that is reflected in other programs as well, that residential education need not be destructive of families, nor does it necessarily separate children emotionally from their parents. They believe that it supports families by making it possible for their children to get the best possible education. In the historical context, residential education is sought after by parents in Israel. The Boyar students are motivated because they are intelligent and have been labeled as gifted by being selected for the program. They want to live up to their reputation and to their potential.

The educational curriculum includes the standard one from the Ministry of Education, but students also have the opportunity beginning in 11th grade to tailor their coursework to their own interests with specialized, advanced "study streams" in literature, Arabic, social sciences, geography, biology, chemistry, and physics. The level at which teaching occurs is reflected by an example from one English classroom, where the teacher guided the discussion of a book by Flannery O'Conner by asking the group to think about the historical context of the early 20th Century Deep South in the United States and to apply that knowledge to the interpretation of the book, a complicated hermeneutical task for high school students for whom English is a second language and to whom American society is relatively unfamiliar.

With regard to the question of discipline, staff members seem unable to understand the possibility of any need for external control and punishment. What might have been defined as misbehavior by outsiders is viewed differently by the staff, and student motivation, self-discipline, and responsibility are simply assumed. Thus, commonalities are evident between this setting and those described above, even though the Boyar students represent an elite group in marked contrast to the youth in most of the other settings, who would be likely to be severely stigmatized if they were in analogous facilities in the States.

Conclusion

One anecdote might be helpful to encapsulate how even severely troubled and troubling young people seem to be viewed in the Israeli settings. Chaim Peri, the director of Yemin Orde, received a call from an Israeli representative in Turkey one day near the end of 1992 to inform him that a Jewish teenager had just crossed the border from Syria, alone, and would be coming to Israel the next day to live–permanently–at Yemin Orde. She did not have an intake file; in fact, there was no additional information about her at all, but she did have a caring community of hundreds of youth and adults who could hardly wait to celebrate her arrival. "Where have you been?" was the message, and one might have added, "We have been waiting for you for almost 2,000 years!" The contrast with the frequent "intake" process and experience in some institutions elsewhere could not have been more stark.

COMPARISONS AND CONTRASTS: SOME EMERGENT THEMES

The following discussion highlights at least some of what seemed to be the most important themes and issues that emerged and energized the participants. They appear to crystallize many of the questions about residential group care in the U.S. that were raised by the comparative experience provided by the seminar.

1. Education versus Care?

In the U.S., what many residential settings for youth provide is called "residential care" or "residential treatment," while in Israel it is called "residential education." Is there a difference? In Israeli programs, the argument goes, care functions must be *developmentally* therapeutic (rather than primarily oriented toward "curing" deficits) and are carried out within an educative environment. Thus, psychologically and sociologically, care is seen as an educational process, so education and care are provided simultaneously. From an Israeli perspective,

> The main task of the educative setting is the intensive transmission of the culture . . . , its concepts, values, norms and spiritual heritage. . . . The orientation is an educational process involving the growth of a complete person, not towards specific "products" such as professions or certain social roles. The use of the residential situation for educational purposes is deliberate; the setting is perceived as a fostering cultural "milieu." The staff, together with the youths who come from the relatively more culturally-established social backgrounds, are accepted as desirable figures for imitation and identification. The stated ideology indicates the intention of transforming children from somewhat marginal social groups (new immigrants

and disadvantaged) into useful citizens. (Smilanski, Kashti, & Arieli, 1982, p. 147)

The distinction between care and education can be a complicated and subtle one even within a single culture; across two cultures, it creates numerous difficulties in discussion and understanding. One implication of the distinction is that the basic conception of what youth in distress need is different. The predominant American approach is technological. For example, one might believe that the primary affliction is emotional, leading to the observed social and behavioral dysfunction. Rehabilitation involves the successful resolution of emotional problems that have their roots in the past–abuse, bad parenting, etc.–and is achieved through clinical "talking therapies." Or one might believe that the problems arise from improper "social learning" and can be corrected through behavior modification.

An alternative is presented, in various forms, by Israeli practitioners and academics. From this point of view, positive development is not achieved through the successful resolution of the past (actually, they would hold, the sequence is reversed) or through the application of a problem-oriented intervention technology. On the contrary, focusing on the problem or the disadvantage leads to further pathology. What is needed first is the absence of the conditions that led to the disadvantage, frequently through removal from the environment (on a voluntary basis if possible) and protection from harm. This process does not seem to be as stigmatizing in Israel as it typically is in the United States, where we often respond to evidence of abuse by involuntary removal from the home and pay less attention to the development-inducing potential of the alternate placement.

Thus, instead of long-term clinical services, communal, educational, and vocational opportunities are offered in an effort to provide the youth with a new "station" in life. At Yemin Orde, this grows from the opportunity to participate in a community. At Hadassim (Levy, 1993b) and MANOF (Cohen, 1986), the focus is on the negotiation of a new identity. Kiryat Ye'arim emphasizes cognitive development through reeducation using the methods that have been developed by Reuven Feuerstein (Feuerstein & Krasilowsky, 1971; Sharron, 1987), which reflect a similar ideological orientation and similar values. Across most of the programs, the common element is voluntary participation and self-determination in an environment where there are clear choices. Sanction-oriented discipline is perceived as counterproductive.

In the U.S., education is conceived more narrowly as primarily cognitive information processing in a school setting. The domain of psychology, despite its history, is conceived as largely separate from education. In Israeli residential education programs, on the other hand, education (pedagogy) is viewed in the more generic, European sense as a cultural process of socialization, and psychological understandings inform both its individual and its collective elements. Schooling is a narrower concept, certainly not synonymous with education.

The differences between these two points of view lead to different questions and answers about the needs of youth. If one believes that resolving emotional conflict or inducing behavioral change are fundamental, the primary focus is on clinical intervention through "talking therapies" or the application of a technology like behavior modification. The young person can remain in the home or, if necessary, be placed in a residential setting that will provide custodial and protective functions. "Schooling" is not the priority–youth can attend "alternative" schools where there is more latitude for behavior and often fewer academic challenges.

If education is viewed seriously as socialization, on the other hand, close attention is paid to all of the influences in the socialization process–the youth's entire world. It may be necessary to remove the youth from environments that are unhealthy–homes that fail to nurture and neighborhoods that tend to socialize in negative directions. The new environment must give consideration to everything with which the child comes into contact. Relationships with adults and with peers, facilities, recreational and cultural activities, and school are means of socialization and must be designed so that day-to-day life encourages rather than inhibits healthy development. This is not, incidentally, to say that all of the elements of the milieu need to be or even should be consistent, as is reflected by the clear distinctions between school and residence environments maintained at Yemin Orde and in related research reported by Eisikovits and Eisikovits (1980).

The interaction between the youth and the environment emphasizes the youth's voluntary participation and freedom of choice in a community with a "dominant ethical attitude" (Levy, 1993a). It is not the application of a technology that effects the change; it is the offer of the choice of a new way of life, reflecting Piaget's (1965) observation that, "The only discipline worth mentioning is that which is freely chosen" (p. 369).

At issue here are beliefs about the nature and significance of trauma and distress, the belief in freedom from vs. determinism by the past, the ontological status of mental health diagnosis, the perceived roles of program and structured discipline, and whether internalization of values and discipline is viewed as the result of the resolution of psychosexual or psychosocial emotional conflicts, the correction of cognitive distortion, existential choice, and/or the attainment of a new identity.

2. Community

Being part of a community can be viewed as restorative in and of itself. In the U.S., troubled and troubling youth are often thought to need something more, such as professional services analogous to medical treatment, to alleviate their problems. If the "illness" or malfunction is not "cured," the individual will continue to have difficulty. In Israel, a community–whether at home or in an appropriate residential placement–is more frequently seen as the restorative means and process that helps the individual to heal and to grow (e.g., Levy, 1996, this volume), and many residential settings are established as largely self-contained quasi-communities rather than as formal institutions.

Community-oriented values are different from "professional" values. For example, the establishment and maintenance of "professional distance" is a fundamental tenet of most treatment-oriented and correctional models in the United States. Most of the Israeli residential education programs, however, appear to see professional practice and the role of professional practitioners very differently. In particular, the concept of professional boundaries is much more limited, as staff and clients interact much more personally and spontaneously. The physical contact between staff and youth noted at MANOF and the "tours" of the Yemin Orde director's quarters mentioned above are but two examples.

Similarly, notions of confidentiality, formal mechanisms to limit agency discretion, and the like are much less salient in Israel–and perhaps less important as well, given the relative absence of stigma connected to participation in the Israeli programs. This appears to be closely linked to their focus on reproducing a community ethos as the core of the program. The implications of this for such programs in the United States, particularly in the light of associated legal and other barriers, need to be explored.

3. Permanence of Commitment

The Israeli programs demonstrate a permanence of commitment to the youth in care and their development. It has been noted that Hadassim and Yemin Orde, and the other programs perhaps to a lesser extent, consider themselves to be primarily communities rather than "agencies." As communities, they and their "citizens" have mutual obligations (Thomas, 1982). For Hadassim and Yemin Orde at least, this commitment extends throughout adolescence and into adulthood. While MANOF is a two-year program, it also supports its students into young adulthood, as needed. In contrast, many U.S. programs find themselves being asked to do more with young people in less and less time and are precluded by funding and other restrictions from providing meaningful support to young people following the residential experience even though such "aftercare" is widely recognized as essential (e.g., see Whittaker, 1992). This difference between the Israeli and American programs is, of course, compatible with the cultural differences between the two societies that have been noted here in other contexts.[8]

4. Social Integration

The Israeli residential settings, for the most part, make a point of being organically linked to the larger community in various ways. Youth from outside may come to the facility to attend school, for recreation, to socialize, and/or for other activities. Youth who live in the settings participate in neighborhood and community events, and most of them shop and some hold part-time jobs outside the residential facility as well.

5. Ideological Commitment

In contrast to the "uprooted" status of many of the youth they serve, Israeli programs mediate a commitment to values and ideals that are rooted in a religious tradition, humanistic or communal values, or nationalistic goals of "building a country." This ideological commitment is experienced and lived on a day-to-day basis and gradually becomes absorbed and accepted by the students, who recognize it as the normative route to a successful life in Israeli society.

There appears to be a purposefulness about the residents of the Israeli programs, perhaps related to this ideological clarity. Individuals know why they are there and what they need to do, not just on a macro-level but on a day-by-day and hour-by-hour basis. Residents are involved in work, in school, and in other activities through which they share a commitment to and interdependence with other people in the community.

Where such an ideological commitment is lacking, as may be the case in many U.S. programs, time is problematic. Whether residents spend their time productively is the responsibility of child and youth care workers instead of the product of a carefully designed environment. Activities are often *ad hoc* and emphasize passive entertainment to keep the youth busy and out of trouble rather than focusing on goal-directed involvement in meaningful, constructive tasks. The result may be a feeling of alienation or existential anxiety that can foster behavioral problems and emotional outbursts.

---

8. This is not the only example that could be cited of a situation where we have reasonably clear research support for the importance of a particular procedure or approach that, nonetheless, we fail to implement.

6. Residential Education as Positive Youth Development

Residential education is widely perceived in Israel as a valuable experience for all youth, regardless of their backgrounds. The setting provides a unique educational and social opportunity, not deprivation or punishment; not the last resort but another chance.

The belief in residential education is associated with ideas of social justice and mobility, access to resources, compassion, and equal opportunity, not just issues of treatment. The question is more than how to "fix" the problems of these young people; it is society's moral obligation to their future. Chaim Adler, for example, reflects this view in suggesting that "economic and social disadvantage is a temporary condition." Residential education is seen as one means of responding to the need to alleviate this condition.

Nor is residential education believed to be destructive of families. On the contrary, it is viewed as providing essential family support. Because the youth is seen as receiving an excellent education in a quality environment, there is less stress in the family. Thus, the placement of a child in a residential program may be a source of family pride and hope, perhaps not qualitatively dissimilar to that of an American from a poor background whose child is admitted to Harvard.

7. Expectation that Change Is Possible[9]

Regardless of philosophy or setting, all of the programs seem to be rooted in the belief that significant change is realistically possible for each youth. This expectation or hope for the future is not just a benign assumption; it is an existential reality that appears to mediate program outcomes as it is reflected in concrete opportunities to participate in legitimate, purposeful work, education, and other social experiences with significant developmental consequences (Beker & Feuerstein, 1991b; Wolins, 1969). Expectancy effects are well documented in the U.S. (e.g., Gergen, 1982; Gumpert & Gumpert, 1968), but the implications of this may be overlooked in residential and other programs in the face of staff pessimism and fatigue and where youth are continually reminded of their problems and failures.

8. Motivation

The Israeli institutions' presumption of motivation on the part of youth is another characteristic that seems to differ from what is the norm in

---

9. The themes described as "Expectation that change is possible," "Permanence of commitment," "Social integration," "Ideological commitment," and "Work" are nearly identical to several of those that Wolins (1969) found to be characteristics of effective group care.

programs in the U.S. In Israel, it appears that motivation is not seen as an individual, psychological trait but is perceived to be socially constituted. This may also be a comment on the crisis of meaning and purpose in at least some parts of U.S. society.

9. The Logic of Misbehavior and Social Control

There appears to be a basic difference between U.S. and Israeli programs in their response to misbehavior; problem behavior may have a completely different significance in Israel. In most U.S. residential settings, such behavior is usually seen as a failure on the part of the youth (and sometimes the institution as well), and the response is usually punitive. In Israel the response may be perceived more as a natural outcome than as a punishment–the youth has made a choice and must live with its consequences. "Misbehavior" is perceived as a mistake, but as only an immediate issue with little long-term significance.

Thus, at Hadassim, MANOF, Yemin Orde, Kiryat Ye'arim, and perhaps in other programs, the behavior that led to placement is perceived not as deviant but as a "rational" response to distress. The solution to the problem, in this view, lies not in the application of rigid rules and structured discipline or "clinical" methodologies to the troubling behavior, but rather in alleviating the distress so that acceptable behavior becomes the "rational" alternative. Such a perspective, it should be noted, is not unknown in the U.S., but it appears to be encountered more often in street youthwork and in academic circles than in residential settings or, for that matter, in the schools.

Some of the Israeli programs indicate that they have no rules, a claim that might meet with a measure of skepticism from sophisticated foreign visitors. What could it possibly mean for organizational discipline that there are no rules? Is this a critical component of the program or an incidental feature? To some extent, the differences may be semantic. The absence of rules does not mean that there are no expectations, exemplified by adults talking to youth about their behavior, the fact that youth are sometimes asked to leave programs, and other consequences for misbehavior that are apparently applied from time to time.

By the same token, however, there appears to be a substantial difference, even if only in degree, in the norms between the two countries with regard to behavioral limits, the social control dimension, and the use of sanctions in residential settings. This appears to reflect a fundamental difference between the two countries in the psychological and philosophical understanding of how youth learn and respond to their environment.

10. Structure, Choice, and Negotiation

The amount of structure provided for residents varies widely, from a high level of structure at Kiryat Ye'arim and in the army program to a relatively low level at Hadassim. What is common across the programs is the possibility for resident choice. Despite the high structure at Kiryat Ye'arim, for example, students can remove themselves from the classroom, suggesting that their time is structured but that their behavior may not be so tightly controlled. Hadassim imposes even less control, of course, and most of whatever structure exists outside the schooling component of the program is created by the residents. Both Hadassim and MANOF view negotiation and choice as primary constituents of the maturation process.

Wozner (1986) posits an interesting relationship between the ideology (or unifying theme) of a program and "negotiation":

> . . . the void left by the lack of a unifying theme may lead to fragmentation of the internat (institution) by the way of individual "ideologies," resulting in alienation and ultimately in revolt or apathy. However, when the lack of a unifying theme is accompanied by a dispersed decision-making process, then a new connecting bond is introduced, namely, the communication of conflicts and consents, i.e., negotiation. (p. 81)

Thus, although the Israeli programs do present clearly apparent unifying themes, an emphasis on negotiation may be one way to cope in settings where such a common purpose is absent. In the U.S., however, tight behavioral control appears to be favored over negotiation as the primary decision-making mechanism at all levels.

11. Multiculturalism

All of the residential programs indicated that they gear their programs to meet the special needs of immigrant and other cultural minority youth, based on the awareness of program personnel that "Israel is a nation of immigrants and we have to learn to get along." The situation is different from that in the U.S. and elsewhere, however, in that the proportion of immigrants or children of immigrants is much higher and most immigrants share at least a religious tradition and often a cultural heritage with the majority population. Most marginal Israeli young people also identify to a greater or lesser extent with the dominant culture, and most of the new-comers have a strong desire to become Israelis. The Ethiopians, for example, see immigration to Israel as the fulfillment of their religious aspirations. Immigrants are also welcomed enthusiastically and, in general, highly valued. Such factors are reflected in the rapidity with which most are able to progress in learning the language. As a result of these factors, Israel (the Arab sector aside) is a relatively homogeneous country, so the implications of the Israeli multicultural experience for more culturally heterogeneous societies are unclear.

Yet the differences and conflicts between Jews of Western origin (Ashkenazim) and those of Eastern origin (Sephardim), as well as Arab-Jewish differences, certainly have implications for a better understanding of ethnic problems elsewhere. One question that seems to be crucial is how the U.S. can define (or renew) for itself the kind of unified, "we're all in this together" perspective that can provide the basis for building a more unified society.

12. National and Cultural Identification

The number of marginal Israeli youth who apparently identify with their country and believe in its ideals was seen as remarkable, expressed in part by their desire to serve in the military. In contrast, such young people in the U.S. seem to be alienated to a degree that Israelis may not appreciate. Soliciting their voluntary participation in residential programs is widely perceived in the U.S. to be an unrealistic approach, since there are few such common denominators or motivational "hooks."

13. Work

Most of the programs have some requirement of constructive work for their residents, including 15 hours per week at Kiryat Ye'arim, which serves younger children. Work is one of the ways youth contribute to–and become part of–the life of the community (Wolins, 1979). By contrast, work as community service has almost disappeared from U.S. programs, except in some specialized settings for delinquents. This happened for several reasons, including liability and other legal issues, labor union opposition, and an admitted history of punishment, exploitation, and abuse of young people in involuntary placement through inappropriate work assignments. Thus, there are good reasons why work has largely disappeared from U.S. programs (and it should be noted that work has become less prominent in many Israeli programs as well), but the young people in care may have lost something useful in the process.

14. *"Official" Requirements*

There appear to be fewer legal and bureaucratic requirements (e.g., detailed reporting) and constraints (e.g., pervasive liability concerns), at least in the formal sense, in Israel than in the U.S. This seems to allow for far greater flexibility in programming. It probably also allows a greater proportion of financial resources and staff time to be devoted to program rather than to administration. Most of all, it allows staff wider latitude to think about what is best for the residents rather than what is permitted by law or bureaucratically feasible. From an American perspective, however, it raises a variety of questions related to accountability and the use and possible abuse of discretion.

15. *A Comparison of Youth Populations*

U.S. residential and other youth-serving programs appear to be experiencing an increase in the number of youth diagnosed with severe emotional and behavioral problems. Some of these young people show little impulse control, are prone to being victimized or victimizing others, are addicted to controlled substances, and/or have a history of violence. It is difficult to ascertain how the Israeli youth in analogous programs compare, although hearing about and observing the freedom that they are given and how they function raises questions about whether the populations are really comparable.

The program whose youth population looks most similar to that in such agencies in the U.S., the ELEM community hostel, is also the program that has the most familiar components and structure–therapy, family treatment, etc. Does that reflect similarities in the youth, or do the youth look similar because the programs are? Kiryat Ye'arim also serves children with admittedly severe problems and has a very structured program, with only about an hour per day free for the residents, but they tend to be considerably younger–junior high school age.

The population of Yemin Orde is comprised mostly of immigrants. While certainly uprooted, many of these young people presumably have personal and interpersonal resources to cope with the transition. As mentioned earlier, they are also motivated to be there and to work toward social integration. Can such youth really be compared to the typical residential care and treatment populations in the U.S.? Few of our new immigrant "unaccompanied minors" are in residential settings.

Smilansky, Kashti, and Arieli (1982) point out that, historically,

> Most of the (Israeli) residential settings . . . serve the needs of the
> average "non-deviant" adolescent of disadvantaged or immigrant

background. They are unwilling to open their educational opportunities for training "deviant" youths. (p. 132)

This could explain the history and role of ELEM and MANOF, in that two different service streams have developed–Youth Aliyah primarily for "normal" immigrant and disadvantaged youth, and programs like ELEM and MANOF for "deviant" or delinquent populations. If this is accurate, Youth Aliyah was able to minimize "treatment" considerations, since a relatively small number of youth had severe psychological or psychiatric problems. Meanwhile, the other programs evolved (as in the U.S.) to cope with more severe problems. It appears, however, that the numbers of more troubled youth are increasing (as seems also to be true in the U.S.), and the Youth Aliyah-type institutions appear to be serving at least some of them in increasing numbers.

Zvi Levy of Hadassim, for example, claims that many of the children there have as severe problems as do those who are elsewhere, and that it is the community of Hadassim that reduces the need of children to act out. He indicates that, despite isolated outbreaks of problem behavior, acting out is not endemic and there is no pervasive abuse of the freedom provided. According to him, the reaction to uprooted youth should not be to use restrictions on freedom as the means of change, but rather to design an environment or community that meets their needs. Levy's (1993b) position that the cause of the distress is relatively unimportant contradicts the tenets of most major treatment ideologies in the U.S.

16. "Charisma"

Is so-called charismatic leadership a key ingredient in the apparent success of the Israeli programs? Certainly each had a director whose performance could be seen in that way, and for each the commitment was more than to a job in the usual sense. Such a leadership model raises questions on several levels, however, including that of transition when necessary, what happens when the leader is away, and more fundamental issues concerning long-term viability and the values that are being modeled for the youth in the program. Yet the success of the programs seems clear, so this question may at least partly answer itself.

17. Similarities in Trends

Arieli (cited in Wozner, 1986) suggests that in Israeli residential programs since the 1950s, there has been

> . . . a decrease in ideological commitment, a change from status socialization to role socialization, an increase in the importance of instrumental goals, decentralization of the organizational structure, increased role differentiation among staff, and an increase in centrality of professional affiliation as the focus of an occupational frame of reference for many staff members. (p. 80)

In other words, the tendency has been to become more like U.S. institutions.

It has already been mentioned that only up until the arrival of recent waves of immigrants, perhaps 1980, was there a trend towards the residential placement of increasing proportions of the disadvantaged (Jaffe, 1986). According to Smilansky, Kashti, and Arieli (1982), a decrease in the demand for residential schools among the non-immigrant student population followed because, although

> . . . they (youth) used to view the residential school almost as their only chance of receiving quality secondary education, they assume today that an equally good education can be acquired in the local schools. (p. 130)

Therefore, fewer mainstream students were choosing to attend residential schools.

Differential diagnosis, with the resulting placement of children in foster care, day programs, and other services, has also decreased the demand on residential programs and has tended to homogenize their populations:

> If differential diagnosis is to be reflected in differential program assignments, a range of appropriate program options must be available. In the absence of such options, workers relied heavily on institutional placement, and diagnoses tended to be tailored to placement realities rather than to clients' needs. . . . As policy directions have emerged with legal and bureaucratic sanctions and evolving support in public opinion, however, a broader range of program options has begun to emerge and to be utilized by those responsible for the critical decisions. (Jaffe, 1986, p. 136)

These trends are significant because they indicate that, as the population eligible for residential programs is defined more like it is in the U.S., the programmatic response is also becoming more similar. This apparent convergence may not indicate, however, that the U.S models are more effective; it may simply reflect the effects of other, less youth-development-oriented influences in both countries, and both may have much to learn from the more traditional Israeli approaches. Perhaps it should also be noted that earlier American residential programs often reflected similar values and orientations (Beker, 1991).

CONCLUSIONS

The deep commitment of Israeli society to the development of children and youth is evident in all the programs, and it is reflected in the seriousness with which the Israelis take their residential services. Yitzhak Kashti of Tel Aviv University notes the importance of the societal context in this regard, suggesting that the following six points should be considered in the process of seeking to understand such services and to compare them across cultures: The historical context ("services develop historically"); the social and economic context of services ("In what context does a service work? What social needs push a service?"); the ideology and beliefs held by the organization; the structure of the service delivery; the evaluation criteria; and the policy options within the particular political context. Thus, it seems clear that residential youth care cannot be separated from the social, cultural, political, and economic contexts in which it is placed.

Therefore, any attempt to apply the lessons of the Israeli experience elsewhere should begin with the development of an accurate understanding of the local context, so that whatever is done will meet the needs of the youth being served and not simply the demands of an external ideology or an irrelevant technology. Nonetheless, while services develop in a historical context, the story of the origin of innovative Israeli organizations suggests that it is possible to create and implement better ways of doing things even–and perhaps even more effectively–in the midst of crisis.

The U.S. is facing a crisis in the development of its youth. At the same time that there is a desire in the child welfare field to focus on community-based services, keeping children in families, and family foster care, there is an increase in the number of children with no families and with disabled families that offer little hope of restoration. In most areas, the foster care system is strained beyond its capacity. Residential programs are one possible response to this crisis, and it seems clear in Israel that, given societal support, such programs can be community- and family-oriented and successful.

Finally, the history of residential education in Israel suggests that, in a climate of danger and despair, retreat and withdrawal are not the only options. While the dangers and the sources of despair are different in the U.S. than they have been over the years in Israel, the Israeli programs demonstrate that it is possible to respond to a crisis with courage and creativity. How we can turn this experience to the benefit of our own programs and our youth depends on the vision and the courage we can muster and incorporate in our own youth services leadership endeavors.

REFERENCES

Beker, J. (1990). Editorial: A cross-national perspective on group care. *Child and Youth Care Forum, 19*(1), 3-5.

Beker, J. (1991). Back to the future: Effective residential group care and treatment for children and youth and the Fritz Redl legacy. *Residential Treatment for Children & Youth, 8*(4), 51-71.

Beker, J., & Feuerstein, R. (1991a). The modifying environment and other environmental perspectives in group care: A conceptual contrast and integration. *Residential Treatment for Children & Youth, 8*(3), 21-37.

Beker, J., & Feuerstein, R. (1991b). Toward a common denominator in effective group care programming: The concept of the modifying environment. *Journal of Child and Youth Care Work, 7,* 20-34.

Cohen, L. (1986). *MANOF: An alternative for the rehabilitation of marginal youth.* Available from MANOF, c/o Dean Chaim Adler, School of Education, Hebrew University, Mt. Scopus Campus, Jerusalem, Israel.

Dewey, J. (1916). *Democracy and education.* New York: Macmillan (Free Press, 1966).

Eisikovits, R., & Eisikovits, Z. (1980). Detotalizing the institutional experience: The role of the school in the residential treatment of juveniles. *Residential and Community Child Care Administration, 1*(4), 365-373.

Eisikovits, Z., & Beker, J. (1986a). Introduction. In Z. Eisikovits & J. Beker (Eds.), *Residential group care in community context: Insights from the Israeli experience* (pp. vii-viii). New York: The Haworth Press, Inc. (Also published as *Child & Youth Services*, 1985, 7(3/4).)

Eisikovits, Z., & Beker, J. (Eds.). (1986b). *Residential group care in community context: Insights from the Israeli experience.* New York: The Haworth Press, Inc. (Also published as *Child & Youth Services*, 1985, 7(3/4).)

ELEM. (1992). 10th Anniversary Report. New York.

Feuerstein, R., Klein, P., & Tannenbaum, A. (Eds.). (1991). *Mediated learning experience: Theoretical, psychosocial, and learning implications.* London: Freund.

Feuerstein, R., & Krasilowsky, D. (1971). The treatment group technique. In M. Wolins & M. Gottesmann (Eds.), *Group care: An Israeli approach–The educational path of Youth Aliyah* (pp. 140-165). New York: Gordon and Breach.

Feuerstein, R., Rand, Y., Hoffman, M., & Miller, R. (1980). *Instrumental enrichment.* Baltimore: University Park Press.

Gergen, K. (1982). From self to science: What is there to know? In J. Suls (Ed.), *Psychological perspectives on the self.* Hillsdale, NJ: Lawrence Erlbaum.

Gottesmann, M. (1991). Residential education in Israel. In M. Gottesmann (Ed.), *Residential child care: An international reader* (pp. 179-193). London: Whiting and Birch.

Gross, J. (1992). Collapse of inner-city families creates America's new orphans. *The New York Times*, March 29.

Gumpert, P., & Gumpert, C. (1968). On the psychology of expectation in the classroom. *The Urban Review, 3*, 21-26.

Jaffe, E. D. (1986). Trends in residential and community care for dependent children and youth in Israel: A policy perspective. In Z. Eisikovits & J. Beker (Eds.), *Residential group care in community context: Insights from the Israeli experience* (pp. 132-142). New York: The Haworth Press, Inc. (Also published as *Child & Youth Services*, 1985, 7(3/4).)

Ladner, J. (1990). Bring back the orphanages. *Family Therapy Networker, 14*(1), 48-49.

Levy, Z. (1993a). *Canadian WIZO-Hadassim: The village and its educational approach.* Unpublished manuscript, Hadassim, Israel.

Levy, Z. (1993b). *Negotiating positive identity in a group care community: Reclaiming uprooted youth.* New York: The Haworth Press, Inc. (Also published as *Child & Youth Services*, 1993, 16(2).)

Levy, Z. (1996). Conceptual foundations of developmentally oriented residential education: A holistic framework for group care that works. *Residential Treatment for Children & Youth, 13*(3), 69-83.

Linton, T. (1969a). The European educateur model: An alternative and effective approach to the mental health of children. *Journal of Special Education, 3*(4), 319-327.

Linton, T. (1969b). The European educateur program for disturbed children. *American Journal of Orthopsychiatry, 39*(1), 125-133.

Linton, T. (1971). The educateur model: A theoretical monograph. *Journal of Special Education, 5*(2), 155-190.

Neill, A. S. (1960). *Summerhill: A radical approach to child rearing.* New York: Hart Publishing Company.

Piaget, J. (1965). *The moral judgment of the child* (Trans. M. Gabain). New York: Free Press (originally published 1932).

Polsky, H., & Fast, J. (1993). Boot camps, juvenile offenders, and culture shock. *Child and Youth Care Forum, 22*(6), 403-415. (See also pp. 401-402, 417-426.)

Sharron, H. (1987). *Changing children's minds: Feuerstein's revolution in the teaching of intelligence.* London: Souvenir Press (E & A), Ltd.

Smilansky, M., Kashti, Y., & Arieli, M. (1982). *The residential education alternative.* Haifa, Israel: Ach Publishing House.

Soukhanov, A. H. (1992). Word watch. *The Atlantic, 270*(4), 127 (October).

Thomas, B. R. (1982). Guest editorial: A fable. *Child Care Quarterly, 11*(2), 95-96.

Weiner, A. (1986). Institutionalizing institutionalization: The historical roots of residential care in Israel. In Z. Eisikovits & J. Beker (Eds.), *Residential group care in community context: Insights from the Israeli experience* (pp. 3-19). New York: The Haworth Press, Inc. (Also published as *Child & Youth Services*, 1985, 7(3/4).)

Weiner, A., & Weiner, E. (1990). *Expanding the options in child placement: Israel's dependent children in care from infancy to adulthood.* New York: University Press of America.

Whittaker, J. K. (1992). Enhancing social support for high risk youth and their families following residential care. In J. D. van der Ploeg, P. M. van den Bergh, M. Klomp, & M. Smit (Eds.), *Vulnerable youth in residential care: Vol. 2. Social competence, social support, and social climate.* Leuven: Garant.

Wolins, M. (1969). Group care: Friend or foe? *Social Work, 14*(1): 35-53. (Also in Wolins, 1974).

Wolins, M. (Ed.). (1974). *Successful group care: Explorations in the powerful environment.* Chicago: Aldine.

Wolins, M. (1979). Work and the internate. *Residential and Community Child Care Administration, 1*(1), 21-40.

Wolins, M., & Gottesman, M. (Eds.). (1971). *Group Care: An Israeli Approach.* New York: Gordon and Breach.

Wozner, Y. (1986). Institution as community. In Z. Eisikovits and J. Beker (Eds.), *Residential group care in community context: Insights from the Israeli experience* (pp. 71-89). New York: The Haworth Press, Inc. (Also published as *Child & Youth Services*, 1985, 7(3/4).)

APPENDIX

1. Sponsoring Organizations

The National Council of Jewish Women, USA (NCJW), the oldest major voluntary Jewish women's organization in the United States and with a long record of education, advocacy, and community service related to children and youth, was the logical organization to launch a collaborative effort to introduce selected Israeli approaches to group care in the United States for several reasons. Historically, the NCJW sponsored an early, distinguished study of U.S. juvenile justice programs. In Israel, NCJW was largely responsible for the development of one of the flagship residential education programs for marginal youth, MANOF. Finally, NCJW managed the successful "importation" of one of its most widely recognized programs in Israel, the Home Instruction Program for Preschool Youngsters (HIPPY), into the United States, where it is being widely implemented across the country.

The Memorandum of Understanding in Social Service (MOU), implemented under the auspices of the Council of Jewish Federations, was established in 1984 as a bi-national agreement between the U.S. Department of Health and Human Services and the Israel Ministry of Labour and Social Affairs to improve the delivery of human services in both countries through collaborative activities and the exchange of ideas and experiences. The National Jewish Community Relations Advisory Council, a partnership of 13 national and 117 local Jewish community relations agencies, also participated. The sponsoring organizations hope to be able to continue to facilitate the process of enhancing services to children and youth in the United States.

2. Seminar Participants

Dr. Charles H. Beady, Jr., President
Piney Woods Country Life School
Piney Woods, Mississippi

Maxine Beady
Piney Woods Country School
Piney Woods, Mississippi

David Beker, Graduate Student
Wurzweiler School of Social Work
Yeshiva University, New York City

Emily Beker
St. Louis Park, Minnesota

Professor Jerome Beker
Youth Studies Program
School of Social Work
University of Minnesota
St. Paul, Minnesota

Larry H. Bilbro, Unit Supervisor
St. Joseph's Home for Children
Minneapolis, Minnesota

Bernard W. Charles
Senior Executive
The McKenzie Group
Washington, DC

Barry Colvin, Executive Director
Illinois Institute of Military
    and Occupational Studies
Springfield, Illinois

Professor Richard English, Dean
School of Social Work
Howard University
Washington, DC

Marilyn Flanzbaum, Vice President
National Council of Jewish Women
New York, New York

Dr. Karen Fulbright
Program Officer
The Ford Foundation
New York, New York

Heidi Goldsmith, Coordinator
U.S.-Israel Memorandum
    of Understanding
Council of Jewish Federations
Washington, DC

Judith P. Gordon
Executive Director
Essex County Section
National Council of Jewish Women
Livingston, New Jersey

Cristy L. James
Director of Site Development
Methodist Home for Children
Raleigh, North Carolina

Stephen A. Joffe, President and CEO
Concord-Assabet Programs
Concord, Massachusetts

Dr. Samuel M. Kelman
Executive Director
Bellefaire/Jewish Children's Bureau
Cleveland, Ohio

Robert B. Law, Executive Director
Experiment in Self-Reliance
Winston-Salem, North Carolina

Dr. LaVera L. Leonard
Vice President for Corporate Affairs
Home Builders Institute
Washington, DC

Rae Linefsky
Assistant Executive Vice President
Federation Employment
    and Guidance Service (FEGS)
New York, New York

Douglas Magnuson
Research Assistant
Youth Studies Program
School of Social Work
University of Minnesota
St. Paul, Minnesota

Karen S. Nettler
Deputy Executive Director
Baltimore Jewish Family Service
Baltimore, Maryland

Sonia M. Perez
Senior Poverty Policy Analyst
National Council of La Raza
Washington, DC

Ruth W. Popkin, Chair
Youth Aliyah Desk
Hadassah
New York, New York

Professor Jack M. Richman
School of Social Work
University of North Carolina
Chapel Hill, North Carolina

Judy Sherman
National Vice President
Child Welfare League of America
Beachwood, Ohio

Dr. Laval S. Wilson, State District
    Superintendent of Schools
Paterson, New Jersey

Tim Wuliger, Chair
Jewish Community Relations
    Committee of Cleveland
Moreland Hills, Ohio

3. Organizers of the Seminar

Heidi Goldsmith, Co-Convener
Coordinator, U.S.-Israel
    Memorandum of Understanding
Council of Jewish Federations
Washington, DC

Hannah Levin, Co-Convener
Director, Israel Affairs
National Council of Jewish Women
New York, New York

Professor Chaim Adler
Seminar Host in Israel
Director, School of Education
The Hebrew University of Jerusalem
Jerusalem

Rachelle Schilo, Israel Coordinator
Director, National Council of Jewish
    Women, Israel Office
Jerusalem

Dr. Jerome Beker
Scholar-in-Residence
Professor, Youth Studies Program
School of Social Work
University of Minnesota
St. Paul, Minnesota

Dr. Stephen G. Donshik, Israel
    Planning Committee
Director, Israel Office
Council of Jewish Federations
Jerusalem

Professor Elite Olshtain, Israel
    Planning Committee
Director, NCJW Research Institute
    for Innovation in Education
The Hebrew University of Jerusalem
Jerusalem

4. Speakers to the Seminar in Israel

Professor Chaim Adler
Director, School of Education
The Hebrew University of Jerusalem
Jerusalem

Eli Amir, Director-General
Youth Aliyah
Jerusalem

Dr. Mordecai Arieli, Head
Center for In-Service Training
School of Education
Tel Aviv University
Ramat Aviv

Eliezer Art, Director
Northern Youth Division
Ministry of Education and Culture
Haifa

Zippora Ben Zimra
National Coordinator
    of Residential Placement
Ministry of Labour and
    Social Affairs
Jerusalem

Sapriela Ben Ezra, Director
Office of Social Services
Tiberias

Avraham Burg
Member of the Knesset
Chair, Education Committee
The Knesset
Jerusalem

Meir Chovav, Director
Division for Youth Development
    and Correctional Services
Ministry of Labour and
    Social Affairs

Professor Reuven Feuerstein
Director
International Center for the
    Enhancement of Learning
    Potential
Jerusalem

Dr. Sami Geraisy, Chairman
Internal (Arab) Christian Committee
    in Israel
Nazareth

Meir Gottesmann
Director-General (Ret.)
Youth Aliyah
Tel Aviv

Professor Reuven Kahane
NCJW Research Institute for
    Innovation in Education
School of Education
The Hebrew University of Jerusalem
Jerusalem

Professor Yitzhak Kashti
School of Education
Tel Aviv University
Ramat Aviv

Avraham Lavine, Israel Coordinator
U.S.-Israel Memorandum
    of Understanding
Director, Department of
    International Relations
Ministry of Labour and
    Social Affairs
Jerusalem

Dr. Gabi Malka
Haifa University
Haifa

Professor Elite Olshtain, Director
NCJW Research Institute for
    Innovation in Education
School of Education
The Hebrew University of Jerusalem
Jerusalem

Ada Pliel-Trossman, Supervisor
National Supervision Division for
    Service for Women and Girls
Ministry of Labour and
    Social Affairs
Jerusalem

Dr. Tamar Rapoport
Senior Researcher
NCJW Research Institute for
    Innovation in Education
Senior Lecturer, School of Education
The Hebrew University of Jerusalem
Jerusalem

Dr. Eliezer Shmueli
Board Chairman
Society of Advancement
    of Education
Jerusalem

Shlomo Uni, Northern Region
    Director of Educational
    Supervision
Youth Aliyah
Haifa

Dr. Anita Weiner, Chairperson
Council for the Child in Placement
School of Social Work
Haifa University
Haifa

Professor Yochanan Wozner
School of Social Work
Tel Aviv University
Ramat Aviv

Note: The authors have endeavored to make these lists accurate and complete and apologize for any errors or omissions that may have occurred. All listed titles and affiliations are as they were at the time of the seminar, January 1993. Speakers affiliated with the settings visited, who generally interacted with the seminar participants more informally, are not listed here but are in some cases identified in the text above.

The Convergence of the Israeli and the European Experience: Implications for Group Care Services in the United States

F. Herbert Barnes
Liese Barnes

SUMMARY. One argument against importing practices from group care programs in other countries is that they are effective and meaningful only in the context of a specific culture and thus have little value for U.S. programs. It is argued here that many Israeli and European practices in such settings are functionally similar to each other, in their emphases on development, community, and identity, and different from the focus on deviant behavior that characterizes many U.S. programs. The key issue is not cultural differences, however, but what is good for children and youth. What could be learned from Israel and Europe is the importance of a professional definition of child and youth care work that takes moral and social values about children seriously in structuring group care programs. *[Article copies available from The Haworth Document Delivery Service: 1-800-342-9678.]*

F. Herbert Barnes and Liese Barnes are affiliated with the International Learning Exchange in Social Pedagogy (ILEX), c/o Youthorizons, Inc., 85 Exchange Street, P. O. Box 15035, Portland, ME 04112. They have worked closely with Socialpedagogs/Educateurs and their teachers from ten different countries of Europe and with the American agencies in which ILEX places these European youthworkers to introduce the concept of Socialpedagogy directly to American thinking and practice. In preparation for writing this article, they also lived briefly in an Israeli youth village, visited several others, and met with leaders of Israeli youth-serving programs.

[Haworth co-indexing entry note]: "The Convergence of the Israeli and the European Experience: Implications for Group Care Services in the United States." Barnes, F. Herbert, and Liese Barnes. Co-published simultaneously in *Residential Treatment for Children & Youth* (The Haworth Press, Inc.) Vol. 13, No. 3, 1996, pp. 49-62; and: *Residential Education as an Option for At-Risk Youth* (ed: Jerome Beker and Douglas Magnuson) The Haworth Press, Inc., 1996, pp. 49-62. Single or multiple copies of this article are available from The Haworth Document Delivery Service [1-800-342-9678, 9:00 a.m. - 5:00 p.m. (EST)].

49

In 1970, when the designation "child care worker" was emerging as a more current and relevant job title than "houseparent" in residential child and youth care programs, a group of mental health, residential treatment, and child welfare professionals–including clinicians, administrators, federal agency heads, and foundation executives–traveled to Switzerland to attend a conference of an international association of "educateurs." Educateurs represent a profession developed in Europe after World War Two whose practice is based in the daily life milieu of group care programs and whose focus is on enhancing development rather than on treatment. The delegation visited agencies where educateurs worked and institutes where they received their professional education.

The educateur developed as a new profession in France after the war when the traditional, leisure-time worker orientation was not adequate to cope with the complex needs of war-ravaged, often displaced and orphaned children; their needs (for nurture, human care and concern, education, even re-education) were so encompassing that there was no opportunity to look at them individually and see them as "disturbed" even if there had been a cultural inclination to do so. So the French concept of the educateur was, one might say, culturally idiosyncratic.

Yet soon the French educateur became the socialpedagog in Holland and Denmark, the barnevernpedagog in Norway, and the Sonder Erzieher in Austria, among others. (In this article, the term "socialpedagog" is used to refer to all of them.) By 1954 a trans-European association of these workers had begun which brought unity to this profession and its practice (Ness & Mitchell, 1990). Meanwhile, professional developments in the United States were moving toward emphasizing individual approaches. Problems were conceptualized as individual, not social malfunctions, and professional approaches oriented toward curing individual pathology were seen as those requiring truly professional skills. The highest order professionals were treatment specialists, not developmental generalists, thus making it natural to see the generalist as indigenous to another culture. In addition, Wolins (1974) identified American cultural proclivities that contribute to the impression of cultural incompatibility, although some of these differences may have become less pronounced in the several intervening decades.

The visits inspired great enthusiasm as the group watched educateurs working in the life-space of the youth and observed their preparation in professional education experiences designed to develop their knowledge, skills, and attitudes–a "professional self"–for competent management of their practice in the milieu of children. Members of the group asked, "Why can't we do this in the United States? Why can't we have workers like this?" But they quickly supplied their own contrary response: "The Educateur is culture-bound. It's fine for France, but it wouldn't work in the U.S."

Twenty years later a similar group journeyed to Israel to study Israeli residential education, as reported by Beker and Magnuson (1996) in this volume. Certainly Israeli residential education is as different from the normative American approach as are European programs developed and operated by educateurs and their counterparts in other countries. Nevertheless, or as a result of the differences, considerable interest in the approach, style, and results of the Israeli programs emerged and was followed by some enthusiastic planning to begin to import this exciting product to the U.S. But there was also a core of reserve that said, "It's culture-bound. It can work in Israel, but it's a product of its culture and would not work for us in the U.S. We are too different, and so are our kids."

There is substantial reason for viewing Israeli residential education as culturally idiosyncratic as well. Israel has large residential schools, each serving hundreds of children and youth, where each direct-care worker (in Hebrew, "Madrich") may be responsible for a "dormitory" of forty children; this would be unacceptable in the U.S. A director who knows all of the several hundred children as individuals, and about whom they say, "He's concerned about us, and he loves us" would be unusual and viewed as "old fashioned" and perhaps even "unprofessional" here, where the director has other "more important" things to do.

ARE ISRAELI AND EUROPEAN APPROACHES CULTURE-BOUND?

An open system where children make daily choices about their activities, their food, their punctuality, and the responsibility they take for the community around them, while being governed by a few very general rules, would be seen here as chaotic. More familiar is a strict schedule and preplanned activities with a strictly maintained staff-child ratio to assure "proper coverage," believed to be necessary because of the level of disturbance of the children. It seems that there must be strong cultural influences underlying these differences. But culture-bound? This paper examines that assumption in greater detail and explores options for looking more inclusively at what we can learn abroad.

SIMILARITIES BETWEEN EUROPE AND ISRAEL

The Israeli residential facility that was studied most thoroughly for this article, Hadassim, a "residential community," appears in many ways to be representative in ideology and approach of such programs in Israel. This community, near Netanya–a small city north of Tel Aviv–includes four major areas: The children's residential houses (twelve large, attractive, centrally located dormitory buildings housing forty children each in ten bedrooms); a staff residential area at one end of the campus with cottages housing couples and their children (about 60 families); the school (which serves almost all 500 residential children and 1000 day students from the surrounding area); and "public buildings" (dining hall, theater, shops, meeting rooms, canteen, offices, etc.).

The director defines the task of Hadassim as to create an "identity-forming environment": "The attempt to run a system whose purpose is identity formation with administrative efficiency creates a lot of activity but very little educational effectiveness" (Levy, 1993, p. 2). "Rather," he says, "we have to find a way to reconcile our legal and administrative obligations with the developmental need of the child for life in a dynamic community" (p. 36). More specifically,

> The village structure and organization aim to provide a set of expectations for a young person, indicating the boundaries of his present identity as well as the identity towards which he is expected to develop. Expectations enable the youngster to test his achievements, or at least his recognized achievements thus far. (Levy, 1993, p. 51)

Levy (1993) also poses a danger that needs to be part of the exploration into commonalities and/or differences among the approaches of the three (or more) cultures:

> A therapeutic environment offering an endless list of bipolar activities in which the child is always the receiver [of treatment and guidance rather than being a participant in mutual interaction] and the adult (as good as he may be) is always the giver will eventually create 'institutionalized' children. (p. 117-118)

While Israeli residential education in all these aspects is a derivative of its culture and could easily be thought to be culturally idiosyncratic, the programs staffed by socialpedagogs in Europe have some very similar parameters. Simply defined, social pedagogy is: *Joint action (staff and persons being served); in the milieu; using activities (from details of daily life to special events) to promote growth and development.* Thus, social pedagogy speaks, as does Israeli residential education, to some common elements that are perceived to be of critical importance:

1. *A Developmental Orientation.* The focus is on helping people to grow and to become more competent in the context of respect for normal boundaries and age appropriate expectations;
2. *An Experiential Orientation.* People learn from experience, and therefore it is the purpose of the worker to provide positive, growth-producing, competency-building experiences;
3. *Quality of Life.* This includes concern for the environment, for interpersonal interactions and transactions, for the tone and content of the milieu, for the respect of all people and their unique identities; and,
4. *Relationships.* This is the medium through which all of the complex processes at work are actualized.

Yet while the programs built by socialpedagogs in Europe as well as the programs in Israel, which express a national commitment to youth development and the youth's importance to the future of the country, have much in common; together, they evidence considerable difference from programs in the U.S. It is these differences that have been cited by U.S. visitors as so much a product of the cultures abroad that the models they have generated have little practical value for enhancing group care programs in the United States.

DIFFERENCES BETWEEN THE U.S. AND ISRAEL/EUROPE

What elements in our culture bind us in such powerful ways that our typical response to these "foreign influences" is to brand them as "culture-bound" and, therefore, virtually irrelevant to our situation and needs?

Twenty-five years ago, sociologist Phillip Slater (1970) observed that three natural human desires are deeply and uniquely frustrated by American culture:

1. The desire for *community*–the wish to live in trust and fraternal co-operation with one's fellows in a total and visible collective entity;
2. The desire for *engagement*–the wish to come directly to grips with social and interpersonal problems and to confront on equal terms an environment that is not composed of ego-extensions; and
3. The desire for *dependence*–the wish to share responsibility for the control of one's impulses and the direction of one's life (quoted in Resnick, Harris, & Blum, 1993, p. S4).

Michael Lerner (1992) proposes that American culture frustrates and denies these elements because of our "misguided emphasis on individuality, which frustrates the deeply felt yearning for connectedness between people that serves to create meaning and happiness in the context of an interdependent community of human beings" (p. 11-23). Yet providing for these desires is fundamental in European and Israeli programs.

VanderVen (1995) sounds the alarm about a more specific danger in the American ideology of group care and in American group care practice–behavior management-focused approaches–which she regards as "another way to fail children."

> Point and level systems to manage behavior seem to be endemic today in group and residential care. Like strange bacteria that can thrive only by being attached to a particular host, they almost seem to float through the air, drop, and install themselves in settings for children and youth, spreading and coming to serve as the focal point for the ideology, activity, and rules for daily living within these agencies.
>
> Point and level systems seem to be a uniquely North American phenomenon. Trained European socialpedagogs . . . coming to work here are stunned and appalled. These practices do not exist in their countries.

So the Israelis define the task as residential education and the Europeans utilize social pedagogy, while U.S. programs focus on residential "treatment" and behavior management. Possibly each of these approaches is culturally determined, but perhaps the field in the U.S. is not irretrievably bound by its escalating emphasis on pathology and deviance and the accompanying focus on behavior and the need to control it: to reinforce it (when we see it as positive); to extinguish it (when we see it as negative); but above all, to quantify it, to measure it, and to use the data to "prove" that the costs of residential treatment are justified. The entire system supporting the field has evolved so as to emphasize such variables as criteria for legitimacy–whether through eligibility for third-party payments (government or insurance), program certification, legal sanctions, or other "official" approvals.

NEW DATA: A WAY OUT

Although this emphasis has burgeoned to the point that the means sometimes seem to be usurping the purpose, Resnick, Harris, and Blum (1993) focus on "the impact of caring and connectedness as protective, nourishing factors in the biographies of young people" (p. S4). The authors state that "much of scientific inquiry in adolescent health has traditionally focussed on the correlation of problemness or pathology. Here a focus on resiliency means that inquiry is directed toward understanding *success* and *well-being*, identifying these factors that buffer against the stresses of everyday life that might otherwise result in adverse physical, social or psychological outcomes for youth." The study notes that a repeated finding has been "the centrality of caring relationships between children and adults" (p. S4).

The study analyzes questions of critical intervention points and, of course, highlights the value of early intervention, and it also notes that while their analysis identifies "caring and connectedness as essential components of health promotion, love alone cannot rectify a lifetime of neglect. Caring, while extraordinarily important in the lives of young people, is not a substitute for correcting fundamental threats to health rooted in the economic disparities that have become manifest" (p. S7).

While the study goes on to emphasize that preventive measures "must remain an enduring goal for pro-child and pro-family policy," it also addresses the question of "what package of interventions will be most effective beyond the point of primary prevention, when young people have already embarked on behaviors that seriously increase the likelihood of 'rotten outcomes'?" (p. S7). But here is the point of fundamental difference between ourselves, Europe, and Israel. The "package of interventions" all too often fails to meet the basic developmental needs of youth.

Resnick, Harris, and Blum (1993) derive a conclusion that addresses the issue directly:

> Our analyses indicate that fostering a sense of caring and connectedness between adolescents and adults should be an integral part of interventions designed to promote resiliency and protective factors, increase adolescents' competency and effective functioning, and promote a sense of meaningful place in the world. (p. S7)

"How this should best be done for very high risk youth populations," the authors continue, "frames the preeminent human services delivery question for the 1990s" (p. S7). They then go on to propose a caveat that also seems exactly relevant to the concern of this paper:

> Those who craft and implement interventions to reduce the quietly disturbed and acting-out behaviors must also deliberate on how and whether the elements of their interventions address the underlying need for adolescent belonging. With the urge toward connectedness representing one of our deepest human desires, caring as a con-

scious, explicit quality must pervade the people and programs that seek to optimize the life course of adolescents, particularly those at highest risk. (pp. S7-S8)

This is true not only for treatment programs, but also in the daily lives of adolescents and youth across the spectrum of youth-serving organizations. It represents an American perspective, from three American investigators, with public and establishment private funding, but its conclusions are completely consistent with European/Israeli program perspectives–and contradict much of what U.S. programs are doing, as noted before. The challenge is clear: Whether through a direct-care milieu professional, as in Europe, or through an interdependent community of people, as in Israel, these countries provide more of what young people need than does the U.S. Whether in socialpedagog-based programs or in residential education centers, the Europeans and the Israelis give more love, more security, more opportunity for expression, more opportunity for relationships, and more opportunity to learn through day-to-day experience and to test oneself in experience and relationship, while U.S. programs–for "troubled" and "normal" youth–seem to be increasingly focusing on behavior–on controlling it, managing it, charting it, quantifying it. The latter concerns dominate plans for service, accountability, staff-child interactions, conferences, supervision, and direct interventions with children. Increasingly, programs are in the behavior business rather than the development business.

WHAT CAN WE LEARN FROM OTHERS?

What contributes to feelings of belonging, which Resnick, Harris, and Blum (1993) have identified, as we have seen, as being so fundamental? Having your behaviors targeted and counted and earning the points for a trip to the movies? Or being involved in a purposeful relationship with a consciously caring adult and a supportive milieu that can offer both nurture and challenge? Which of these contributes to belonging?

It would be incorrect to suggest that Europeans and Israelis are concerned with care and connectedness while Americans are not. But it is, unfortunately, correct to state that these countries have built professional and/or programmatic approaches to address those concerns and, in the main, the U.S. has not. Instead, the U.S. has developed an ever-increasing preoccupation with social control and superficial behavioral change (e.g., as reflected in the accumulation of "points") and programs that operate more and more mechanically without explicit evidence of care, connectedness, and building a sense of belonging. This has evolved over time and for a variety of reasons, including the interests of the dominant professions (those centered on the illness orientation), funding streams (who pays for what), the pressures of "managed care" and accountability (what has been produced), liability issues, and hierarchical organizational models (in which low-level milieu staff are required to be other-directed rather than responsible for the exercise of independent judgment).

Toward a Professional Definition of the Work

But the most salient reason for the inadequacy, from our point of view the one that dominates all others, is the failure to have developed in the U.S. a professional definition for the work that should be taking place directly in the here-and-now of the residential milieu. Lacking that, work in the milieu is often regarded simply as *managing* (directing) the routines of daily living: When daily life is perceived as merely routines to be managed, workers "will inevitably have to use coercion and exercises of power to get children to do these 'prescribed and detailed courses of action'" (Barnes, 1991, p. 137). The Israeli and European programs demonstrate, essentially, how much better it would be were workers empowered to use the activities of daily life educationally; thus, "what workers ought to be talking about and planning and working on with children is the managing of the essentials of daily life as a total activity, demanding joint action and full involvement of children and staff members because it's our place, and therefore, it's our project" (Barnes, 1991, p. 138).

When workers taking care of children have neither the autonomy (or "space") nor the professional resources (e.g., appropriate knowledge and skills) to do things in planned ways so as to make them participatory and educational, things quickly devolve into just managing behavior and controlling the group.[1]

The work that should be taking place directly in the here and now of the residential milieu is well described elsewhere in this volume by Zvi Levy (1996), the Director of Hadassim, who says that "most critical to the development of a cohesive identity is the opportunity to experience personal autonomy in a wide range of interpersonal interactions within a flexible educational setting. Reality is tested and grasped through *negotiation* with real people, in real situations, rather than *rigid laws*" (cited in

---

1. In the hands of non-professionals, it should be noted, "managing behavior" becomes something quite different from those forms of behavior modification that provide a conceptualized and credible methodology appropriate for use in operating a residential program.

Beker & Magnuson, 1996, this volume, p. 10). Levy is referring to the opportunity he visualizes for any of the children at Hadassim. Without a doubt, what he is describing is also grist for the mill of the educateur or socialpedagog.

Unfortunately, this does not reflect the experience of children in most U.S. residential treatment centers or the kind of relationship a child is likely to have with his child care worker, who may be working almost mechanically on the basis of rules and procedures set down from above. Unfortunately for the child who would profit from an empowered relationship with a direct care worker, this worker is carrying out rules directed primarily toward management, control, and maintaining the prescribed routine–the "structured setting" made necessary by the children's presumed high level of disturbance.

But Hadassim also accepts children from very troubled families, from dangerous situations, from the streets–kids who lack "controls from within" and who certainly would be seen there (and in many European settings) as needing external controls. But the kinds of controls that are seen as needed are as varied as the kinds of primary prevention discussed earlier. Levy is talking about internal controls that "arise in the context of the acknowledgment of legitimate authority rather than through the use of regulations or coercion" (Beker & Magnuson, 1996, this volume, p. 11).

How can an institution of 500 residents, from the ages of about 6 to 18, boys and girls, little kids and vigorous young men and women, exist harmoniously in a situation where there are few punishments or losses of privileges, no concentration on behavior or misbehavior, and where the staff's primary means to control behavior is "persuasion and negotiation"? There are no automatic sanctions, except in response to breaking the "law of the land"–e.g., theft, drugs, assault. There are no levels, no points, no token economy or "behavioral store," essentially no restrictions, no earning your way to a trip with "good" behavior or being kept home because of "bad" behavior.

European professionals who work in the U.S. as participants in a technical, professional exchange program (ILEX) are always concerned about the formulaic responses that they frequently observe. They are particularly concerned with physical restraints that they report being used even in such episodes as outbursts of anger or verbal disagreements. So, too, they experience the same feelings when they encounter behavioral points, level systems, mandatory activities, restrictions, and loss of privileges. The ILEX Fellows conclude that Americans are unduly preoccupied with managing and controlling children and unwilling (or unable) to allow them to experiment and to experience themselves and the impact of their own ideas.

So what do these European and Israeli professionals do and think about instead? Levy (1993) states that over the course of several years a youth at Hadassim has to make thousands of decisions in the context of daily living and

> Each time, he or she must assess reality, make a judgement about how to act, and accept some responsibility for the consequences. In order for this to produce developmental change, the organization needs to be designed to provide a reality that supports the young person in making such choices and dealing with their consequences, through which a new identity emerges over time. (Beker & Magnuson, 1996, this volume, p. 11)

French educateurs in U.S. agencies as ILEX Fellows have consistently posed a conflict with the normative American way of thinking about how to deal with a group. They will often be heard to say: "Je propose un activite." Their American colleagues understand this as too non-directive. But it is not a matter of literal language translation; it is a matter of literal professional practice transfer: "I propose an activity to the kids. Maybe they want to do it, maybe they don't. Maybe some do. It's O.K." That is not casual and irresponsible, as many Americans are so quick to think. It is not enough to say, "Well, that's French!" The Norwegians do it, too. They would no more think of forcing an activity on a child than the French do. It is a matter of attitude and definition of purpose.

The tools of Israeli direct care workers are discussion, persuasion, and negotiation. The socialpedagogs' tools are relationship building and pedagogical action in the context of a recognized, professional role and function. The Americans' tools are schedules, programs, management, control, and punishment. Why? Are we all culture-bound? And, if so, what binds U.S. culture to make American direct care workers look like prison wardens while European and Israeli cultures allow their workers to look like educators?

ILEX Fellows over the past eleven years have uniformly observed that they get along well with American youth. Are American kids more troubled, more disturbed, than in France? The idea that they are is usually the Americans' explanation for the totality of structure that the European professionals find so limiting. (This argument, that U.S. programs deal with more difficult young people, may be fruitless, since such definitions themselves may be culturally linked, but it is clear that there is at least a great deal of overlap among the populations involved–certainly enough to justify the attempt to extrapolate appropriately from the European and Israeli experiences.)

Additionally, these foreign professionals attest to their astonishment with what to them is a horrifying level of violence in the culture—not only on TV on a daily basis, but also in the interactions among people and in the lack of respect on the part of children for adults and on the part of adults for children, including issuing orders and not including children in discussions of decisions that pertain to them. In that sense, "Je propose . . ." probably does reflect a cultural as well as a professional difference.

But what if non-violence, respect for others, consideration for others' ideas and feelings, group discussion, team discussion, joint action of staff and children, and using the daily-life milieu as a nurturing, friendly laboratory for learning life's tasks of cooperation and self-actualization were all woven together and made part of a conscious and explicit unifying orientation? Might it then be more possible for controls to, in Levy's words as cited previously (p. 58), "arise in context of the acknowledgment of legitimate authority rather than through the imposition of regulations and coercion"? But in order to have that, it is quite obvious that some specific ingredients that currently appear to be in short supply in group care in the U.S. must be present.

First, there must be a cultural belief that youth are important. In Israel they truly are regarded as the future of the country. Most will be going into the army for three years or more to defend the country, and they are expected to be active nationalists and productive citizens in a cooperative, interdependent culture, so they know that they are needed. In Europe, there is explicit recognition of youth as citizens and as persons of interest and value with whom it is important and worthwhile to communicate.

In the U.S., on the other hand, there is frequently a marked difference between what is said about the value of children and what is done to them in education and social services. This often extends to actual fear of adolescents, seeing them primarily as threats–to persons, to institutions, to the *status quo*. But there is the possibility that we could conceptualize programs around the importance of adolescents as persons and as learners, not just around changing their behavior.

In Israel, the nature and quality of programs seem to be extensions of national beliefs, so it is not surprising that residential services are conceptualized as education rather than as treatment, and that conceptualization seems to make a significant difference in what takes place. In Europe, the definitions of program and practice are now an outgrowth of the socialpedagogical profession. These professionals place high value on relationship (staff-child, child-child, staff-staff) and on joint action ("Je propose"). Program elements (activities, daily life events, trips) are developed by the practitioners *with* the children and are designed to meet multiple goals (group building, education, fun, cultural development, knowledge about place and identity). Accountability is achieved through team reflection, which involves self and peer criticism and conscious review of goals and accomplishments, and establishes targets as well as specific immediate and long range plans.

CONCLUSION

It is interesting to observe how both Europe and Israel get to essentially the same place through different means. In Europe, it is through the profession of social pedagogy. In Israel it is through the system and ideology of residential education. Unfortunately for residential care in the U.S., however, there is neither. Mired in a morass of regulation, dominated by the demand to produce quantifiable results or face the loss of funding, caught in highly developed structures organized to do the wrong thing while being primarily concerned with managing and controlling those who should be helped and educated, U.S. residential programs are understandably defensive. But programs abroad do suggest how more viable alternatives might be developed despite apparent cultural discrepancies, if we have the will and the skill to do so.

In spite of what we know or, as has sometimes been said, *because* of what we "know," we have a lot to learn.

REFERENCES

Barnes, F. H. (1991). From warehouse to greenhouse: Play, work and the routines of daily living in groups as the core of milieu treatment. In J. Beker & Z. Eisikovits (Eds.), *Knowledge utilization in residential child and youth care practice* (pp. 123-155). Washington, DC: Child Welfare League of America.

Beker, J., & Magnuson, D. (1996). Residential education as an option for at-risk youth: Learning from the Israeli experience. *Residential Treatment for Children & Youth, 13*(3), 3-48.

Lerner, M. (1992). A platform for the politics of meaning: A value-oriented approach to progressive politics. *Tikkun, 7*(4), 11-23.

Levy, Z. (1993). *Negotiating positive identity in a group care community: Reclaiming uprooted youth.* Binghamton, NY: The Haworth Press, Inc. (Also published as *Child & Youth Services*, 1993, *16*(2).)

Levy, Z. (1996). Conceptual foundations of developmentally oriented residential education: A holistic framework for group care that works. *Residential Treatment for Children & Youth, 13*(3), 69-83.

Ness, A. E., & Mitchell, M. L. (1990). AIEJI: Creating a profession to work with troubled children and youth. *Child and Youth Care Quarterly, 19*(3), 199-207.

Resnick, M. D., Harris, L. J., & Blum, R. W. (1993). The impact of caring and connectedness on adolescent health and well-being. *Journal of Pediatric Child Health Supplement, 1*, S3 to S9.

Slater, P. (1970). The pursuit of loneliness: American culture at the breaking point. Boston: Beacon Press.

VanderVen, K. (1995). Point and level systems: Another way to fail children and youth. *Child and Youth Care Forum, 24*(6).

Wolins, M. M. (1974). Group care: Friend or foe? In M. M. Wolins (Ed.), *Group care: Explorations in the powerful environment.* Chicago: Aldine.

Some Implications
of the African-American Experience
for the Development of Residential Education
in the United States

Richard A. English

SUMMARY. Residential education as practiced and organized in Israel (Beker & Magnuson, 1996a; Levy, 1993; Levy, undated), if appropriately adapted and culturally sensitive, is suitable for serving the needs of minority children and youth, particularly African Americans, in the United States. Although this approach differs systematically and significantly from most current residential services for at-risk youth, it has much in common with traditional programs that facilitated the development and socialization of African Americans in the late Nineteenth and early Twentieth Centuries. *[Article copies available from The Haworth Document Delivery Service: 1-800-342-9678.]*

In a recent report on youth policy and services commissioned by The Carnegie Council on Adolescent Development through its Task Force on Youth Development and Community Programs, Michael Sherraden (1992) examined community-based youth services in the United States in international perspective. Based on the study of youth policy and services in Australia, Germany, Norway, Sweden, and the United Kingdom, he con-

---

Richard A. English is affiliated with the School of Social Work, Howard University, 601 Howard Place NW, Washington, DC 20059.

[Haworth co-indexing entry note]: "Some Implications of the African-American Experience for the Development of Residential Education in the United States." English, Richard A. Co-published simultaneously in *Residential Treatment for Children & Youth* (The Haworth Press, Inc.) Vol. 13, No. 3, 1996, pp. 63-67; and: *Residential Education as an Option for At-Risk Youth* (ed: Jerome Beker and Douglas Magnuson) The Haworth Press, Inc., 1996, pp. 63-67. Single or multiple copies of this article are available from The Haworth Document Delivery Service [1-800-342-9678, 9:00 a.m. - 5:00 p.m. (EST)].

cluded that their community-based services for adolescents 10 to 15 years of age in these five countries tended to be "developmental, broadly based, inclusive and participative" (Sherraden, 1992, p. ix).

In the United States, on the other hand, he points out, youth services and policy tend to be directed toward the remediation of individual difficulties rather than broader youth development and socialization. Additionally, youth services in the U. S. context–especially institutional youth services–are heavily influenced by a mental health ethos, although many of those under the sponsorship of voluntary agencies tend to address socialization and developmental issues as well. However, these services are unevenly available to American children and youth and do not serve large numbers of poor and minority children (Sherraden, 1992, p. ix).

RESIDENTIAL EDUCATION IN ISRAEL

Youth services in Israel are similar in purpose and character to youth services in the five Western European countries described by Sherraden. Their major focus is on education and youth development, rather than on mental health deficits and treatment of children and youth. This was evident in the course of a ten-day seminar in Israel in which I participated in 1993, as is described and analyzed in the volume of which this article is a part (Beker & Magnuson, 1996b), which included discussions with educational leaders and university scholars, practitioners and policymakers, and visits to seven residential centers among the many there that together serve more than 50,000 children. These centers serve a wide range of young people of junior high school to senior high school age who are living in extra-familial circumstances, including immigrants, gifted children, slow learners, children in trouble with juvenile authorities but without formal convictions, and socially deprived children.

There is no social stigma attached to residential education in Israel as there is in many other parts of the world; going away from home to a residential center for learning has deep roots in traditional Judaism, and the Holocaust left many children displaced and in need of permanent alternative care arrangements. An important goal of these centers is to bring youth from the margins into the mainstream and to facilitate their integration into the Israeli society as productive citizens. In addition, in 1993 there were over 800 Arabic children in education residential centers, all of which were under Christian auspices.

From my own observations, residential education centers in Israel are places where children and youth are valued. They are safe and secure environments that are nurturing and where children can develop unfettered. Leadership in the centers tends to be charismatic and antibureaucratic. These centers are highly mission-oriented. Great time, effort and planning have been devoted to creating the "perfect" organizational climate for education and healthy development and socialization. There is a strong emphasis on preserving ethnic identity, rather than a melting-pot approach to cultural differences.

ECHOES OF THE AFRICAN-AMERICAN EXPERIENCE IN ISRAELI RESIDENTIAL EDUCATION

There are striking parallels between the Israeli residential centers and the Black experience in the United States. In the absence of institutionalized child welfare services for African American children (Billingsley & Giovannoni, 1972; Peebles-Wilkins, 1995), many of the historically Black colleges and universities (HBCUs) founded in the aftermath of the American Civil War and the Emancipation Proclamation of 1863, which freed the enslaved Africans, incorporated residential education for grade school and high school students in their structures (DeLauder, 1990). In many cases primary and secondary education was the principal education offered. Like the immigrants to Israel, the former slaves and their children found themselves in comprehensive residential settings where the individual was valued and cherished. The analogy reflects that both groups came from unsafe environments to places where one could be in harmony with oneself and one's world.

As these institutions matured and the numbers of qualified college-age young people increased, their instructional programs in primary and secondary education declined. They were eventually phased out and closed as public education became available to African American youth in the southern states. A similar fate befell the private boarding schools for Blacks that had been designed not as collegiate institutions but as secondary schools.

Other similarities between the African American and Israeli residential settings include the quality of the institutional leadership and the commitment to education, youth development, and socialization. Both approaches are highly mission-oriented and view the task as building strong individuals and a strong society simultaneously, by rediscovering and reconstructing cultural roots.

Another analogy between the HBCUs and the Israeli residential centers lies in the "technology" favored in both settings. Both focus on the students' minds, education, and developmental needs. Deficits, deviance, people-processing, and treatment are not addressed directly nor included in the technological system.

In the HBCUs, there was a "fit" between school and family, something we heard less about in Israel, although family contact and involvement seem to be valued; the amount of contact with one's family may be less, but its importance is just as great. Still, there are essential tasks that residential schools can accomplish that families cannot. Despite the importance of debureaucratization, Weber was right—bureaucracies house expertise, which is often needed. But programs need to work appropriately with the family, which requires individualization on the basis of needs and resources; it is not just a matter of sending notes home and the like.

Children are often the primary culture-bearers (in both directions) between the family and the larger community, particularly for families in transitional or rapidly changing social environments, e.g., immigrants and former slaves. Family-sensitive residential education, such as that provided by the Israeli programs and the HBCUs, may be particularly significant in this connection.

Ethnic identity issues are also involved. The HBCUs allowed young black people to flourish in a somewhat protected environment and to be prepared to enter the wider society, just as the Israeli settings appear to be doing for that society's newer subcultural minorities, such as the Ethiopian Jews.

The objectives of both of these sets of programs are clear and similar, directed toward the upward social and economic mobility of the young people being served through the development of self-confidence and competence in the context of a realistic understanding of the societal context in which they are to live their lives.

THE ROLE OF THE STAFF

The roles of social workers and other professionals in these settings transcend and frequently replace the traditional emphasis on clinical services in settings for marginal youth—indeed, one of the elements they share is that they do not regard or treat the youth as marginal at all, but rather as perhaps needing to be "retrofitted" with essential skills they did not attain earlier and the confidence that they are, indeed, not marginal despite the contrary messages that may have come from their earlier lives.

Thus, the required professional skills emphasize planning, organization, and the administration and management of these kinds of environments, as well as the specifics of working sensitively and creatively to empower the youth involved. They include the skills and commitment needed to link appropriately with families and to help young people and their family members to link with one another. They also need, most importantly, to be able to provide the kinds of appropriate, developmentally-oriented socialization experiences that enable young people to explore and respect who they are, ethnically and otherwise, where they came from, their uprootedness, and what they want to do with their lives. Zvi Levy says, "Don't tell a child what to do; tell him who he is!" (Beker & Magnuson, 1996a, p. 11). Maybe this is the process we used to call "guidance."

It should be noted that this is not the kind of work that can be done in a 50-minute hour or an eight-hour day, no evenings and weekends. It requires the kind of commitment that keeps workers "available" to youth–physically and psychologically–as needed, and often involves their families as well in providing support, modeling "normal" life, etc. It did the job in the historically Black colleges and universities and appears to be doing so in the residential education settings in Israel. These experiences can do much to guide us as we seek to build successful interventions for marginal youth in the United States as we approach the Twenty-First Century.

REFERENCES

Beker, J., & Magnuson, D. (1996a). Residential education as an option for at-risk youth: Learning from the Israeli experience. *Residential Treatment for Children & Youth, 13*(3), 3-48.

Beker, J., & Magnuson, D. (Eds.). (1996b). Residential education as an option for at-risk youth. *Residential Treatment for Children & Youth, 13*(3).

Billingsley, A., & Giovannoni, J. M. (1972). *Children of the storm: Black children and American child welfare.* New York: Harcourt Brace Jovanovich, Inc.

Delauder, W. B. (Ed.). (1990). *Leadership and learning: An interpretive history of historically Black land-grant colleges and universities.* Washington, DC: U.S. Department of Agriculture.

Levy, Z. (1993). *Negotiating positive identity in a group care community: Reclaiming uprooted youth.* Binghamton, NY: The Haworth Press, Inc. (Also published as *Child & Youth Services,* 1993, *16*(2).)

Levy, Z. (undated). Individual and group care in residential settings: The Israeli scene today. Unpublished manuscript.

Peebles-Wilkins, W. (1995). Janie Porter Barrett and the Virginia Industrial School for Colored Girls: Community response to the needs of African-American children. *Child Welfare, LXXIV*(1).

Sherraden, M. (1992). *Community-based youth services in international perspective.* Washington, DC: The Carnegie Corporation.

Conceptual Foundations
of Developmentally Oriented
Residential Education:
A Holistic Framework
for Group Care that Works

Zvi Levy

SUMMARY. In rehabilitative residential settings in the United States, there is a strong tendency to address mainly the young residents' lack in knowledge and skills while giving them psychotherapeutic support. Such programs also tend to give primacy in their mode of organization to operational efficiency. Thus, they often overlook the disruption of the child's or adolescent's developmental process, a disruption that cannot be mended satisfactorily in an institution organized primarily for operational efficiency, didactic educational processes, clinical therapy, and behavioral control. What is needed is a growth-supportive community that minimizes messages of deficit and maximizes messages of possibility to the child; a community life pattern in contrast to an institutional life pattern; a planned environment in contrast to planned activities; a child's basic experience of choice in contrast to the requirement of obedience; and a lifestyle that confirms belonging and destiny in contrast to alienation and fate. *[Article copies available from The Haworth Document Delivery Service: 1-800-342-9678.]*

Zvi Levy is affiliated with Hadassim Youth Village (a project of Canadian WIZO), Hadassim 42 845, Israel.

[Haworth co-indexing entry note]: "Conceptual Foundations of Developmentally Oriented Residential Education: A Holistic Framework for Group Care that Works." Levy, Zvi. Co-published simultaneously in *Residential Treatment for Children & Youth* (The Haworth Press, Inc.) Vol. 13, No. 3, 1996, pp. 69-83; and: *Residential Education as an Option for At-Risk Youth* (ed: Jerome Beker and Douglas Magnuson) The Haworth Press, Inc., 1996, pp. 69-83. Single or multiple copies of this article are available from The Haworth Document Delivery Service [1-800-342-9678, 9:00 a.m. - 5:00 p.m. (EST)].

69

In the organization and direction of residential settings, there is an unfortunate tendency to ignore the extensive knowledge that has been accumulated on the subject. Somehow, there seems to be a feeling that it is a simple matter to establish alternative life frameworks for children and youth who need them. "Everyone" knows how to raise children. "Everyone" knows what services they need and where to find the experts to provide them: dietitians, clinical specialists, experts on leisure activities such as sports and music, and so forth. What is too often ignored is the need for experts on living itself, if it is to be organized artificially. As a result, such programs tend to be structured for administrative and operational efficiency rather than for their potency in promoting youth development.

One of the more harmful results of this tendency is the reliance on simplistic images and hypotheses whose sources are notional and not theoretical, such as the idea that a homeless child needs something that *looks* like a family, creating the image of "a warm little home" with a small number of adults taking care of a small number of children. An elementary theoretical analysis shows that what a homeless child needs is something that *behaves* and *feels*–to the child–like a family, not simply something that looks like a family from the outside. In today's circumstances, most "warm little homes" that are not natural families–and even many that are–do not and cannot behave like families in this deeper sense.

What *can* behave like a family is a *community*. A "warm little home" cannot, by itself, give the young person adequate conditions for proper development, but a community of a few hundred children and adults can (Levy, 1993). The crucial components of such commmunities are presented in the sections that follow.

LIFESTYLES FOR YOUTH DEVELOPMENT

Although many eminent thinkers, including Bettelheim (1950), Bronfenbrenner (1979), Erikson (1950), Feuerstein (Feuerstein, Klein, & Tannenbaum, 1991), Maier (1987), Postman (1979; Postman & Weingarten, 1969), and Redl (1966) have emphasized the need for programs to focus on the developmental requirements of their clientele, children and youth needing alternative homes are still being placed in group care environments that are organized so as to provide an efficient combination of services at the expense of supporting youth development. Among the components typically organized in this way are:

1. Accommodation services and their attendant needs: Food, security, hygiene, and leisure;

2. Teaching services and their attendant needs: school, teachers, and equipment; and
3. Physical and mental health services. (The latter are usually dominant in residential settings, because they are regarded as necessary in working with young people in distress.)

Little thought is given to the overall way of life created by such a combination of services, or to the fact that the way of life, or lifestyle, is what determines the child's developmental and identity-formation processes. At least in part, this is the product of the demands of the task as defined in the setting. For example, is it all right for the staff to show feelings or is that "not professional"? Are they habitually tense and brusque in their interactions, or are they usually calm and relaxed? What annoys them and what makes them happy? What is forgivable and what is not? What is regarded as important and what as trivial? If the lifestyle does not suit the child's or adolescent's developmental needs, the entire enterprise will not work, just as any human framework that does not match its participant's identity needs will not work (Cushman, 1990).

What is needed, therefore, is to replace the thinking that guides the organization and direction of residential settings on the basis of the most efficient organization of services with an emphasis on organizing such settings as environments supportive of development, using the needed services as means to an end rather than as the goal of the residential setting. The organization of the right mode of life must be the focus, and every other activity of the residential setting should be subordinated to this consideration.

THE DEVELOPMENT OF COMMUNITIES
FOR THE DEVELOPMENT OF INDIVIDUALS

To establish a program in this way, all of the factors that comprise the residential setting or affect it must be taken into account, including, among others, the following:

1. The character of the population of youth in the setting relative to the make-up of the general population;
2. The distance of the residential setting from population centers and the potency of the stimuli (positive and negative) that exist in those centers;
3. The social values prevalent in society at large;

4. The message that the youth infers from the fact that his family and his "world" sent him to the residential setting;
5. The availability of telephone contact and transportation;
6. Access to the media and the strength of their influence;
7. Development of care professions and modalities of therapeutic intervention;
8. The professional diversity and degree of specialization of the staff; and
9. The variance in ethics and guiding orientations among staff who have varying backgrounds and are members of different professions.

The focus in program development is not on changing *parts* of the life of the residential setting or on the addition of new parts, but on principles for organizing the setting as a whole, the "Gestalt," in such a way as to create the desired mode of living. Thus, the task is to design and implement a community lifestyle, as reflected, for example, in the design and construction of facilities, the choice of equipment, the selection and training of staff, the choice of student population (numbers, ages, personal traits, cultural characteristics, etc.), the daily routine, the role of the school in the young person's life, the range of activities offered outside the school, the place of psychotherapeutic workers in the resident's life, the administrative routine (ways of communication, division of authority and responsibility, degree of precision in defining roles, patterns of leadership, etc.), the residential community's connections with the external human environment, and its connections with the ideological environment of the surrounding society.

Youth Development vs. Operational Efficiency

The conceptual framework for organizing a residential setting as a community oriented toward youth development versus organizing it for operational efficiency will be presented as a series of structural and psychosocial conceptual continuums. Some of the key *structural* components of residential frameworks, for example, appear in Table 1. Each variable can be viewed as a continuum on which a particular setting's position can be seen as influencing its position on the "umbrella" continuum of Youth Development vs. Operational Efficiency.

If we compare the two kinds of frameworks from a *psychosocial* perspective, a different set of variables emerges, such as those portrayed in Table 2. Combining these two domains, we can see that a multi-age and coed environment with a wealth of constructive, contributory roles and activity opportunities, for example, provides a greater range of stimuli

TABLE 1. Structural Characteristics of Residential Frameworks

A Residential Framework Emphasizing the *Development* *of a Community*	A Residential Framework Emphasizing *Operational* *Efficiency* ("Institutional")
A few hundred residents	A few dozen residents
A wide age range	A narrow age range
A coed population	A single-sex population
Length of stay unlimited in advance	Length of stay limited in advance
Openness to the environment	Seclusion from the environment
A rich variety of activity opportunities	A limited variety of activity opportunities
Cultural heterogeneity	Cultural homogeneity
Easy access to information about the residential environment	Limited access to information about the residential environment

than one that is homogeneous in terms of age and sex and limits itself to a smaller number of opportunities for participation. An environment that allows and encourages the people who live in it to have unlimited access to most of the elements that compose it tends to confirm a sense of acceptance and to decrease feelings of rejection. These are all elements of healthy families as well as developmentally oriented communities.

In the development of these structural and psychosocial characteristics as the basis for a coherent program, attention must be given to the psychosocial meaning of the simplest elements of life in the residential setting: the location of the dormitories and the staff quarters, the routes people move along by virtue of their occupations and activities, the design of the windows and doors in the dormitories and other facilities–these (and countless others like them) determine the extent of the young people's access to information about their world. Rules and procedures regulate only a limited portion of the flow of such information.

The orientation of a group care program–whether emphasizing youth development through community or operational efficiency–is reflected not

TABLE 2. Psychosocial Characteristics of Residential Frameworks

A Residential Framework Emphasizing the *Development of a Community*	A Residential Framework Emphasizing *Operational Efficiency*
A wealth of stimuli	A paucity of stimuli
Possibilities of spontaneous reactions to stimuli	Blocking of spontaneous reactions to stimuli
An environment whose elements are easily comprehensible to the youth	A confusing environment whose elements are not easily comprehensible
A reasonable prospect of completing a process, however long, without the threat of a "deadline"	The feeling of being threatened by a "deadline," which acts as an impediment to the prospect of completing the process
Availability of worthy objects for imitation and identification	Absence of objects worthy of imitation and identification
A lifestyle that confirms a feeling of acceptance	A lifestyle that confirms a feeling of rejection
A lifestyle that confirms a sense of belonging	A lifestyle that confirms a sense of alienation
A lifestyle that confirms a sense of destiny that is chosen, or at least consciously accepted, by the youth[a]	A lifestyle that confirms a sense of fate, over which one has no control[b]

[a]This is connected with a sense of Vocation, a feeling that one is committed to the achievement of set goals (whatever they may be).

[b]The situation here is one of determinism. This state of mind works to avoid activity and seeks social invisibility as a preferred survival strategy.

only in the subjective experience of the residents, but also in the influence of the setting on their development. An environment emphasizing elements that appeal to the youth's "strong" side and not to his or her "weak" or "flawed" side confirms a sense of belonging and destiny and weakens a sense of alienation and fatalism.

Elements that appeal to the weak side tend to link to operational efficiency and include, for example, areas that are out of bounds ("In certain places you can't be trusted to behave properly"), staff whose main occupation is enforcing discipline ("In certain matters your judgment can't be trusted and your behavior needs to be controlled"), and even professional "treatment" people such as psychologists and social workers if their presence is conspicuous and dominant. Elements that appeal to the strong side tend to facilitate personal and social development and include, for example, sophisticated activities, frequent opportunities to represent the residential setting outside, and so forth.

Pedagogic vs. Didactic Leadership

Leadership patterns in group care settings tend to reflect and do much to determine the overall orientation of the setting. What might be called "pedagogic" leadership emphasizes human development in a community context; "didactic" leadership is directed more toward operating efficiency. Table 3 contrasts some of the characteristics and consequences of pedagogic leadership in a community-oriented residential setting and those emphasizing didactic leadership in the context of operational efficiency.

Organizational and Experiential Implications

In order to build an environment supportive of growth as a process of (1) weaving together the accumulation of abilities, knowledge, and skills, and (2) organization of psychosocial identity, we must take into consideration the possibilities defined in Table 4. With full awareness of the meaning of the choice, we should choose the pedagogic leadership side of the various sequences if we seek to focus a group care environment on human development.

SPECIAL CONSIDERATIONS
IN THE DEVELOPMENTAL PROCESS

We cannot determine the time or the force with which the strong needs of identity formation will be revealed. The body and its organs, physical strength and mental ability, motor skills, sexuality, the need to live in a social context–all these and many more will harmoniously coexist only if the youngster is strongly attached to a human group whose way of life he gradually deciphers with the growth of his own ability to understand and participate. We can determine, therefore, according to the way in which we organize the youth's life environment whether his identity-forming process will occur within the overall context of the prevailing culture or whether he will need to seek a way out of his internal disorder through the coordinates of a deviant subculture.

The harmonious existence of the components of identity also depends

TABLE 3. Characteristics and Consequences of Pedagogically-Oriented Leadership vs. Didactically-Oriented Leadership in Residential Frameworks

Categories	The *Pedagogic* Conception	The *Didactic* Conception
Conception of Adolescent Development	Growth as a process of integration	Growth as a process of accumulation
Responsibility for Failure	Failure of the process is perceived by adults as *deprivation of* the residents	Failure of the process is perceived by the adults as *deficits in* the residents
The Optimal Framework for these Processes	Human life cycle	Functional organizational frameworks
Developmental Mechanisms Reinforced by the Conception	A. *Unconscious imitation* as a development-promoting mechanism (spontaneous imitation of adult behaviors, until the youth's general behavior finally becomes adult) B. *Identification* with significant adults as a stage in identity development (with gradual adoption of values)	A. *Half-conscious imitation* as a way to relieve anxieties (mechanical imitation of "ideal" adult when, in fact, there is no way to imitate a "hero" of this or any other kind). The imitation is designed to soothe in situations of confusion and anxiety. B. *Solidarity* with similar figures as an anxiety soothing mechanism (frequently based on negation of adults' values)
Adolescent's Subjective Experience	A. A reassuring and invigorating sense of identity B. A sense of positive identity ("I'm significant in my world because of my good qualities.")	A. Feelings of anxiety B. A sense of negative identity ("I'm significant in my world because of my bad qualities.")
Coping Mechanisms Reinforced by the Lifestyle	Psychological *adjustment* mechanisms (partly conscious) coping with external reality, until a reassuring sense of identity is achieved	Psychological *defense* mechanisms (unconscious) coping with elements of internal reality, in an attempt to soothe an unresolved conflict

TABLE 4. Organizational, Experiential, and Developmental Implications of the Two Orientations

Parameter	Organization of a *Growth-Supportive* Environment	Organization of an Environment that Perfects *Behavior Control*
Organization of the Environment	Theoretical basis: Pedagogic (the thinking that guides reconstruction of an environment supporting psychological development) Optimal lifestyle for development and consolidation of identity Community life pattern (a goal-directed group, in which everyone, at all times, may influence the definition of the goal, the internal order of priorities, ways and means of reaching the goal, and the main aspects of the lifestyle) A precisely planned *environment* (planning of the activity in the hands of the people living in the environment)	Theoretical basis: Didactic (the thinking that guides imparting the knowledge and skills needed for action in foreseeable future consequences) Efficient combination of accommodation, teaching and counseling services, and professional psychological support Institutional life pattern (a goal-directed organization, in which most of the people, most of the time, have no chance of influencing the spheres mentioned here) *Activity* planned in detail (each part of the activity planned in advance and dictated to the people living in the environment)
Structuring of the Basic Experience	Basic experience: *Choice* 1. Independent judgment of reality 2. Action according to personal decision 3. Coping with the new reality	Basic experience: *Obedience* 1. Accepting the other's judgment of reality 2. Action according to external order 3. Evaluation of results by outside opinion
Nature of the Most Frequent Conflict	Double positive choice (+/+) Positive/negative choice (+/−)	Double negative choice (−/−)

(continued)

TABLE 4 (continued)

Parameter	Organization of a <u>Growth-Supportive</u> Environment	Organization of an <u>Environment that Perfects *Behavior Control*</u>
Most Frequent Psychological States	Productive tension (invigorating) Self-focused experience (self-examination as a person *within* a group)	Anxiety (paralyzing) Outer-focused experience (self-examination as a person *vis-à-vis* a group)
Pattern of Development	Spiral integration in an overall living environment. (The spheres of develop-ment and its pace are determined by mutual stimulus/response of the individual and the world around him.)	Linear growth on a track of acquiring knowledge and skills. (The spheres of development and its pace are determined by pressure and the reward/punishment relations of the individual with the world around him.)
Motivational Dynamics	Mechanisms of community recognition (feeling of failure: *Guilt*, which is the sense of someone who was given responsibility for others or for his world, and failed. Adults experience guilt feelings.)	Mechanisms of formal approval/permission (feeling of failure: *Shame*, which is the sense of someone who was given a simple and mechanical task and did not perform it properly. Small children often feel shame.)
Quality of the Adolescent's Lifestyle	*Experiential:* Expression of strength; emotion in interpersonal context Participation in problem solving team (experiences of interdependence, changing with the change in personal quality and sense of identity) Communication as two-way negotiations (competing with the other's strength) *Tentative access* in four spheres: People, time, space, technology[a] Activity as an expression of positive identity	*Exercises:* Mechanical functioning in dictated task context; mechanical functioning in dictated social context "Participation" in exclusive pattern of receiving (experiences of uniform and unchanging dependence) Communication as one-way listening (giving up competition in advance) *Dictated activity* in four spheres: People, time, space, technology[a] Activity "therapy" as an expression of negative identity

(continued)

TABLE 4 (continued)

Parameter	Organization of a Growth-Supportive Environment	Organization of an Environment that Perfects Behavior Control
Qualities of the System from the Viewpoint of the Child's Psychology	*Borders* of individual liberty (created through interaction among people, events, ideas; dynamically changeable)	*Limits* of individual liberty (limits defined in advance for each person, event, idea, etc.; can be changed only by formal process)
	Life pattern *analogous* to prevailing culture (arena for development of existing potential and formation of future identity, in the context of an increasingly comprehensible reality)	Life pattern *alternative* to prevailing culture (arena for correction of faults that cast doubt on the nature of the future identity, in the context of an incomprehensible reality)
	Mechanisms of marking horizons (methodical approach to potential accumulated in the past, in the context of future realization)	Mechanisms of soothing anxieties (methodical approach to faults accumulated in the past, in the context of immediate relief)
	Moratorium as responsible and active waiting (the contact with adults and the link to their world continue, although outright demands are not made of the child)—the youngster still "belongs."	"Moratorium" as temporary removal of responsibility by the adult (the contact with adults and the link to their world disappears, together with the disappearance of outright demands for certain behaviors)—the youngster does not "belong" at this time.

aTechnology refers to the technology of everyday life. One of the characteristics of children in distress is loss of the ability, or of the inner belief in one's right, to make use of the technology of everyday life. For youngsters in a residential setting such simple matters as using a knife, locking the door of their room, having access to their own pocket money and choosing how to spend it, and access to electrical appliances become questions of "law," of administrative efficiency, and so forth. This has an enormous effect on the youngster. In our world, people draw a large part of their sense of worth from the technology that they are capable of using and have the right to use.

on the maintenance of a significant degree of continuity from past to future, as well as the availability of "occupations" (roles or "stations" in the community), generally technological and integrally related to the group and its ongoing history, whose demands enable the youth to test his growing abilities, commitment to the community, and, simultaneously, his changing social status.

This is a set of conditions that cannot easily be communicated didactically, if at all; it can be achieved only by turning the entire residential setting into a goal-directed community characterized by a majority commitment to the following:

1. The goal;
2. The order of fundamental priorities;
3. The ethos;
4. Willingness to recognize at least some of the youth's qualities as assets to himself or herself and to the community;
5. Willingness to enable the young person to experience motor skills, intellectual skills, and social skills, individually or together with the community, as she or he chooses, while simultaneously enabling the individual to be in touch with his or her emotional needs;
6. Willingness to grant the young people a moratorium from the normative demands placed before youngsters of their age, while not "walking out on them";[1]
7. Willingness to allow the young residents free access to knowledge concerning the actions of the community;
8. Willingness to allow the youth to evaluate the results of his actions through the experience of emotional feedback, power and influence, and status and prestige; and
9. Willingness to maintain a life pattern analogous to that prevailing in the mainstream of the prevailing culture.

---

1. According to Erikson (1968), a moratorium means exempting the youngster from certain obligations while keeping him a full member of his societal group. The exemption is partial and temporary, and while the borders of the partial and temporary are not formally defined in advance, they are marked minutely by the lifestyle of the group (for example, by the fact that none of the older members enjoy that moratorium unless they are labelled as the village idiot, the village clown, etc.). The youngster who is granted a moratorium knows that it is a temporary situation; he knows that he belongs to the group and that as he gets older he will continue to be a member of that group although he will no longer be able to behave as he did during the moratorium period, when he was growing and developing. Thus, the concept of moratorium should in no way be confused with abdication.

This kind of community can be created if the residential setting is organized with a strong bias towards the left side of the parameters presented in Tables 1 to 4. Once created, its lifestyle supports positive identity development among the residents. This appears to have been the situation in the "classic" Israeli youth villages in the first decades of their existence. By introducing many of these elements, their leaders succeeded in creating a lifestyle that reduced to a minimum the youth's clashes with the world and were capable of containing emotional outbursts when clashes did occur.

But the classic youth villages had an advantage that most residential settings do not enjoy today, in that the young people involved did not generally face the dilemma of choosing between identity outlines. Their parents and other significant figures in their lives before they came to the youth village led a way of life similar to those of the adults they encountered in the setting. Therefore, the process of organizing their identities according to the parameters of behavior, intellectual and aesthetic standards, and emotional and moral preferences that began in their original environments could continue uninterrupted by major lifestyle and identity disparities.

It may not be possible to change completely the basic identity components of a young person who comes to a residential setting after having been exposed to contrary influences for many years. Unless the youth has rejected them, parents and other significant figures from the lifestyle to which he or she has become accustomed are by then too formidable as established objects of identification to permit wholesale change. Therefore, it is necessary to begin from the stage of identity formation in which the youth is functioning when she or he arrives and to navigate carefully towards the desired goals.

CONCLUSION

In helping the child to solve the complex dilemma of identity, we can organize our services on the basis of operating efficiency or, alternatively, on the basis of support for positive identity development.

Organization Based on Operating Efficiency

A lifestyle resulting from a combination of services guided by considerations of operating efficiency conveys messages to the young person in either of two unacceptable ways:

1. I'll end up like my parents, because I'm criticized and disapproved of, like them. I'm at the bottom of the social ladder, like them. My chances of acquiring power and expressing emotion exist only in the context of protest and disruption, like theirs.

It should be emphasized that these messages are not communicated to the youngster verbally. The verbal messages repeatedly transmitted may even be the opposite, but what counts is what is conveyed by the lifestyle. This identity outline acts as a self-fulfilling prophecy and results in the well known phenomenon of social reproduction.

2. I must do everything so as not to be like my parents, because those around me show me better ways, so I must imitate them and adopt their world of values.

Here the youth's experiences match the verbal messages conveyed by the adults, but this is a naive revolutionary attempt that has no chance. At best it creates a negative identity, in this case the identity of someone adjusting in spite of himself or herself so as to achieve from the world the material resources and social approbation necessary for his or her existence and mental well-being.

Organization Based on Support for Positive Identity Development

In contrast, a way of life derived from an approach that gives priority to the creation of an environment supportive of positive identity development sketches identity outlines such as the following:

I must be like my parents would have been if they had had the opportunity, because, as I can see from the opportunities that are given to me, I have excellent potential. My parents obviously had the same potential but did not have the opportunity to realize it.

If the developmental environment is constructed appropriately, that is to say, if the youth lives in an environment whose *modus operandi* and its meaning for his or her life are comprehensible, there will be adults around in whom one can easily identify the good and healthy parts of his or her parents.

When these adults become objects of identification for the resident, they will not be in conflict or competition with the identification objects he brought with him to the residential setting. They will be like the familiar ones, except that they live differently because their environment is different. They will be effective objects of identification because the youth understands their way of life and can imitate and identify with it, and because they make no immediate demands to turn one's back on his or her former life or to throw out all of one's existing beliefs and behaviors. Such an outline contains the prospect of identity formation that offers possibilities for social mobility–the identity of one who believes in what has been accumulated so far and feels that he or she has the right and the ability to control his or her fate and to use the assets accumulated to advance toward an emerging series of clear and desired horizons.

An environment that allows the young person to struggle freely with the crises of identity formation also frees a great deal of the energy that might otherwise be invested in solving anxiety arousing conflicts born of endless clashes between the motives acting on the youth in the process of organizing identity and the demands of the curriculum. The available objects of identification stop being a threat to the youth's former identity and a disruption of what he or she sees as worth doing; the pressure caused by the need to "betray" his or her history, parents, and other significant figures is removed. As a result, the youth's chance of integrating improves in a pedagogically oriented program. The accumulation of "assets" is not blocked and organization can be achieved.

REFERENCES

Bettelheim, B. (1950). *Love is not enough.* New York: The Free Press.

Bronfenbrenner, U. (1979). *The ecology of human development: Experiments by nature and design.* Cambridge, MA: Harvard University.

Cushman, P. (1990). Why the self is empty: Toward a historically situated psychology. *American Psychologist, 45*(5), 599-611.

Erikson, E. H. (1950). *Childhood and society* (2nd ed.). New York: Norton.

Erikson, E. H. (1968). *Identity: Youth and crisis.* New York: Norton.

Feuerstein. R., Klein, P. S., & Tannenbaum, A. J. (1991). *Mediated learning experience (MLE): Theoretical, psychosocial, and learning implications.* London: Freund Publishing Group.

Levy, Z. (1993). *Negotiating positive identity in a group care community: Reclaiming uprooted youth.* Binghamton, NY: The Haworth Press, Inc. (Also published as *Child & Youth Services,* 1993, *16*(2).)

Maier, H. W. (1987) *Developmental group care of children and youth: Concepts and practice.* New York: The Haworth Press, Inc. (Also published as *Child & Youth Services,* 1987, *9*(2).)

Postman, N. (1979). *Teaching as a conserving activity.* New York: Delacorte Press.

Postman, N., & Weingarten, C. (1969). *Teaching as a subversive activity.* New York: Delacorte Press.

Redl, F. (1966). *When we deal with children.* New York: The Free Press.

Human Development Imperatives in the Organization of Group Care Programs: A Practical Approach

Douglas Magnuson
F. Herbert Barnes
Jerome Beker

SUMMARY. Bureaucratic organization of group care services has cost us ethically and pedagogically by constraining and demoralizing staff and clients and in the creation and recreation of a direct care practice in disarray. Business management theorists have been struggling with many of the same issues, and it is suggested that new management conceptions point the way towards pedagogical organization that is supportive of human development. Changes will require that we have (1) a conceptual understanding of practice based on line worker autonomy, a collegial working environment, collaborative relationships with clients, and an ideologically oriented program; (2) an implementation strategy for the transition to the new model; and (3) an understanding of how current fiscal realities can accommodate it. *[Article copies available from The Haworth Document Delivery Service: 1-800-342-9678.]*

Douglas Magnuson and Jerome Beker are affiliated with the Youth Studies Program, School of Social Work, University of Minnesota, 386 McNeal Hall, 1985 Buford Avenue, St. Paul, MN 55108. F. Herbert Barnes is affiliated with the International Learning Exchange in Social Pedagogy (ILEX), c/o Youthorizons, Inc., P. O. Box 15035, Portland, ME 04112.

[Haworth co-indexing entry note]: "Human Development Imperatives in the Organization of Group Care Programs: A Practical Approach." Magnuson, Douglas, F. Herbert Barnes, and Jerome Beker. Co-published simultaneously in *Residential Treatment for Children & Youth* (The Haworth Press, Inc.) Vol. 13, No. 3, 1996, pp. 85-97; and: *Residential Education as an Option for At-Risk Youth* (ed: Jerome Beker and Douglas Magnuson) The Haworth Press, Inc., 1996, pp. 85-97. Single or multiple copies of this article are available from The Haworth Document Delivery Service [1-800-342-9678, 9:00 a.m. - 5:00 p.m. (EST)].

To ask the question, "What does supervision cost?" is to assume that the type of supervision–understood in its broadest meaning as the organizational support system–needed for a given population is known and uncontroversial. By not challenging this assumption new programs and new program ideas get swallowed, digested, and emerge looking like programs and services that have gone before. The underlying assumption, as Levy (1996, this volume) points out, is that bureaucratic resolutions of the problem are foundational, and that pedagogical and ethical issues have to live within these established bureaucratic parameters. This bureaucratic definition of supervision and program has cost us ethically and pedagogically by constraining and demoralizing staff and clients and in the creation and recreation of a direct care practice in disarray.

Levy (1993; 1996, this volume) argues persuasively that it is possible to implement a child and youth care work that is organized pedagogically–that is, based on sound principles of growth and development–rather than bureaucratically. This conception turns traditional Weberian bureaucratic ways of thinking (MacIntyre, 1984) inside out and, in so doing, addresses some of the ethical dilemmas of bureaucratic management, undercuts the pathological features of organizations, and converts objections to change based on the assumed immutability of "what is" into opportunities for creativity and inquiry into "what might be."

Those who work in residential group care settings often hear and repeat the bromide that such programs are the least desirable alternative for young people but are, unfortunately, necessary for some given the sad condition of their lives. Given this attitude, it is of little wonder that residential programs are so often drab, depressing, and uninteresting environments that do more to reinforce than to change the defeatist perspectives of their young clientele. In short, many of these settings are boring and distasteful, and every contact with them leaves us feeling unclean.

Still, we tend to brace ourselves as we conclude that, since they are necessary, we had better run our programs as efficiently as possible. Thus, organizational theory was imported into social services in good faith, with the hope that ". . . organization was the key to improving the delivery of services to children and their families" (Thomas, 1994, p. 13), but the consequences both for employees and for clients have been harmful. A brief discussion of emerging thinking in organizational development and management may help to clarify why and point the way toward practical approaches to constructive change.

THE REDISCOVERY OF HUMAN DEVELOPMENT
IN MANAGEMENT THEORY

The premises of traditional business management theory have long been challenged by those who recognize that management practices have not been producing either worker satisfaction or increased productivity. Thus, management theory is coming to terms with the realization that there is a "conflict between the formal structure of human organizations and the psychological needs of human individuals" (Hardy, 1991, p. 146). The principal issue is that traditional methods of management, with efficiency as their goal and employee control as their means, are undesirable because they are both ethically objectionable and counterproductive. The needed change, according to the critics, is that organizational management should be thought of as a context of human development.

Management theory is principally concerned with the management of "normal" adults in employment settings; the residential group care programs being discussed here serve children and youth, primarily those who are viewed as incapacitated in some way, and as clients rather than as employees. Is there any justification for the connection between management practices and the clients, beyond the management role of the staff? It is our thesis that the formal structure of many residential programs not only works against the development of the employees–for reasons that will become clear–but also impedes the development of the children and youth being served. This article and the volume in which it appears demonstrate that such consequences reflect the imposition of inappropriate management ideologies and are, therefore, not inevitable.

IMPLICATIONS FOR RESIDENTIAL GROUP CARE PROGRAMS

Ethical Concerns

The ethical objection to traditional management theory and principles of bureaucratic life is straightforward:

> The manager represents in his *character* the obliteration of the dis tinction between manipulative and non-manipulative social rela tions. . . . The manager treats ends as givens, as outside his scope; his concern is with technique. . . . (MacIntyre, 1984, p. 30)

Managerial technique is used with the goal of inducing employees to increase productivity towards the achievement of the organizational goals.

These goals are not questioned by the manager, and employees are not allowed to question them, even though they are value-laden.

Instead, managers and employees focus their energies on effectiveness, the ultimate bureaucratic criterion of value, which is "inseparable from a mode of existence in which the contrivance of means is in central part the manipulation of human beings into compliant patterns of behavior; and it is by appeal to his own effectiveness in this respect that the manager claims authority within the manipulative mode" (MacIntyre, 1984, p. 74).

Thus, when management as effectiveness is separated from the social purpose and ends, it becomes a raw exercise of power, and persons are treated as means to an end. It is this that is so objectionable about traditional management and about the practices of many child welfare agencies. Psychology–and raw power–are used as to manipulate children and workers to comply. Drucker (1974) argues against this "psychological despotism," believing that it violates the principle of respect for persons, and suggests that what is needed in organizational life is a reconfiguration of work so that employees participate in creating their own jobs, their own work, their own goals, and, yes, living with the consequences, performance and otherwise.

In the case of children and youth, if we accept the premise that the ethical principle of respect for persons is violated by many "therapeutic" interventions with children and youth, then we must find other ways of eliciting the cooperation of our clients than the use of power and control mechanisms and supposedly therapeutic techniques. Of course, there are always situations in which it is necessary to use control in order to protect others, but in most programs the necessity is rare.

Harm to Workers

Argyris (cited in Hardy, 1991) argues that persons should be viewed as developmental beings, growing toward autonomy, from short-term interests to long-term interests and goals, and toward increasing self-direction and self-awareness. Formal organizational structures, on the other hand, are typically designed in such a way as to limit growth–to restrict freedom, autonomy, trust, and self-awareness. Thus, the employee experiences dissonance between his or her developmental needs and the demands of the organization. The result is "decreases in production and in identification with the organization; increases in waste, errors, absenteeism, sickness, apathy and disinterest in work, and increase in importance of the material [financial] aspect of work" (p. 148). These factors lead management to blame the worker and to seek better and more efficient methods of control that have the same counterproductive consequences, causing management to blame the worker, and the cycle continues.

Kipnis (1984) suggests that it is not just their performance that affects how employees are treated, but also the way the job is structured. In two studies, managers' evaluations of employees were correlated with the level of the routinization of the employees' tasks. Those whose jobs were more routine tended to be evaluated more negatively; the employee's actual performance did not matter. In another study, Kipnis (1984) found that managers not only evaluated employees in routinized positions more negatively, but also used more manipulative methods of influence with them.

One negative consequence of routinization and of managerial control is what Kipnis (1976) calls the "metamorphic" effects of power. Supervisors are tempted to influence employees' behavior in order to fulfill their own needs. If the employee complies with an attempt to control, the supervisor attributes this to his or her own power and not to the competence or willingness of the target. As a result, the employee's abilities are devalued and the social distance between supervisor and worker is increased. Thus, Argyris (cited in Hardy, 1991) and Kipnis (1987) argue that even routine applications of power and control damage the human development of individuals. MacIntyre (1984) says that powerholders appear to have control, but it is really impotence disguised as power. Executives and managers in child and youth care do not really have as much power as some would like to believe, and what power they do exert over others impacts them in negative ways. A few minutes listening to child care workers or social workers talk about their bosses verifies this observation.

Harm to Children

If traditional management practices are counterproductive and counter-developmental for employees, is it not likely that they are also counterproductive and counter-developmental when used with children? Workers tend to replicate the management style of the organization in their interactions with those they serve. The elaborate motivational systems, the detailed "consequences" for innumerable misbehaviors, and the interminable rules are all components of management systems designed to induce compliance by clients as well as by staff, recalling the analyses of Goffman (1961) and Rosenhan (1973). Such practices tend to have the same effects on children as they have on staff, as noted above. Children feel manipulated and attribute changes in their behavior to the program and the control of the staff, not to their own interests and abilities. Apathy and cynicism increase; staff and children become more distant from each other.

When we look at a residential program's organizational chart, what we often see is a pyramid, with direct care staff at the bottom. Such diagrams are usually organized on the basis of bureaucratic efficiency–Weber's organizational criterion of value–and assume the necessity of close supervision and control of those at the lower levels. From this perspective, clients–for whom the organization supposedly exists–are seen instead as the objects of its control. It is as if the "customer" were viewed as an instrumentality of the organization rather than as its *raison d'être*. Further, in such programs the customer is, in a sense, the "product" as well and needs to be seen as the center or focus of organizational effort, as Barnes (1991) and Barnes and Barnes (1996, this volume) have reported to be normative for residential workers in much of Western Europe.

Programmatic Consequences

In most U.S. residential programs, direct care staff have the least authority, the least education and training, the least recognition, and the least pay. Yet we bemoan our inability to attract quality caregivers. It might be more accurate, however, to suggest that the field includes a far greater share of excellent workers than should be expected, given its record of insensitive micro-management and the overall lack of support for direct care staff. Thus, in spite of the conscientious, loving, intelligent efforts of many caring people who take jobs as child care workers, this work continues to be "the only field you have to get out of to get ahead" (Stuck, 1994).

In spite of the efforts of state and national associations of child care workers, the field continues to be an employment but not a profession–or even, in most cases, a vocation or a career in the full sense of those terms. It can never be that as long as the work, its practice, its hours, and its required preparation (if any) are determined by bureaucratically organized agencies rather than by a professionally defined and regulated critical mass of direct and indirect practitioners who have entered the field through pre-service professional education instead of training. This is especially important if we expect direct care personnel to do complex work in critical and strategic relationships with other people where judgment built on basic good common sense and exercised on a minute-by-minute basis is required.

The desire to change this debilitating situation has been expressed in many ways over many years, but it has persisted as a vicious cycle. An administrator cannot pay a professional salary to a non-professional person in a non-professional role in the hope that such a move will increase the value of the work and thereby begin a process of upgrading it to the necessary level. Yet is it likely that competent professionals will take up work in such settings given present conditions, which effectively preclude using this expertise effectively? Even if professional education for it were available, how many people would spend two or three years in pre-service education to do this complex, demanding work in a professional way at the salaries that child care workers currently receive?

Data from a recent Child Welfare League of America (1993) study indicates that the mean salary for Residential Child Care Workers in the mid-Atlantic region is between $15,000 and $17,000, or between $7.21 and $8.17 per hour. In and of itself, this figure is a defining statement that must be changed and can be, but only in tandem with needed changes in the other elements cited previously. Only thus can the vicious cycle be broken.

The problem described in this section is composed of three parts–the lack of a conceptual model to define what the practice actually is; the lack of an implementation strategy; and the lack of a clear understanding of the fiscal viability of change. To some extent, all three must be addressed simultaneously.

TOWARD A MORE VIABLE CONCEPTUAL MODEL

Traditional management theory is based on a lack of confidence in the line employee and the presumed need to control input and output. In group care this means, as we know, that direct care workers are not respected or even trusted. This is demonstrated by their limited input into treatment planning, their lack of decision-making authority, even about many minor details of program and day-to-day life, their limited access to resources, and the restriction of their opportunities to exercise interpersonal judgment. Although the two examples that follow may seem extreme, they actually occurred and dramatically illustrate the problem.

In one residence where there was a problem with flies, the child care worker was required to keep all of the flies she killed to prove that she was doing something about it. In another nationally known agency, child care workers are not allowed access to additional toilet paper for the bathroom without routing the request through the supervisor. These are not atypical examples of the routine distrust of the line worker that characterizes most group care settings.

Even more counterproductive is the conceptual and theoretical vacuum in which most child care workers are expected to operate. Because the worker has typically not received an adequate professional educational experience, there is little respect and the quality of care suffers. Quality of care is also related to working conditions, which themselves are partially determined by the organizational structure.

Thus, new management approaches that are replacing the traditional, control-oriented hierarchical model with collaborative effort, greater worker autonomy, and more emphasis on education have significant implications for the changes needed in group care programs. This model, sometimes called the "organizational development" (OD) approach, incorporates, among others, these key elements:

- Reliance on group process to guide staff performance in contrast with formal structural properties.
- Mobilization of an action-research model to inform performance in an ongoing way.
- Recognition that the work team is the key unit for using action-research to generate more effective modes of organizational behavior.
- Acknowledgement that collaborative, as opposed to top-down management, is essential to making the model work within the work-team construct. (French & Bell, cited in Thomas, 1994, p. 87-88)

Authority and responsibility are given to the line workers, and the manager's role is to educate and facilitate their development.

It is in fact the manager who must prove his or her worth to the line worker. As White (1995) puts it, "Managers are a tax on the line worker." The manager functions as a skilled educational and resource consultant. The primary authority, though, is not the individual worker; it is the work team composed of direct care workers (not a clinical team). Individuals are accountable to these work teams for their performance. The work team supervises client treatment planning, evaluation of individual team members' performance, management of the daily routine (including maintenance of an environment supportive of development), professional communication with colleagues, and management of routine financial affairs. In short, it is the work team of line workers that is ultimately responsible for the quality of the environment and program. It is, of course, vital that the work team have a well developed conceptual model of practice.

The management principles described here and Levy's (1996, this volume) conceptual model, despite certain cultural differences, suggest how the needed changes might best be approached. First, instead of practices oriented toward coercing behavior change, we would establish structured, collaborative relationships between staff and children and between children and among children, thus inviting participation and eliciting cooperation in common developmental experiences. Control-oriented practices, on the other hand, often lead to perverse competition and power struggles between staff and children, yet we know that development of the character qualities we desire occurs only in an atmosphere of cooperation and mutual support (Johnson & Johnson, 1989). That atmosphere cannot be created in an environment where eliminating negative behavior is the only program rationale. We must learn to be more creative, even with the most difficult children and youth, in implementing non-coercive interpersonal relationships and interventions. Better yet, we must design environments where the need for coercion is less likely.

Second, instead of programs that communicate bureaucratic program model convictions, we would develop programs that are oriented to ideological and moral messages. In many current programs, it is much easier for the children to understand what they are *not* supposed to do than what they *are* supposed to do. A focus on ideological conviction orients activities and behaviors in directions that are consistent with basic values. Transgression of those values is about violating a principle, not a rule, and correcting the problem is not about punishment but about reconciliation and restoration of a relationship.

Third, residential programs would recognize the original, native self-determination of children, even those who have been damaged. Steinberg, Elmer, and Mounts (1989) call this "psychological autonomy," which is easily violated if the focus is on the attempt to stop problem behavior. Self-determination is not the outcome of a program of socialization and treatment; it is an original condition. Youniss (cited in Maccoby, 1992) argues that "socialization should not be described as a process whereby control of children is shifted from adults to the children themselves, who become progressively more autonomous and self-regulated. Rather . . . at every stage of life, relationships involve coregulation . . ." (p. 1014).

What we want to do is help young people to exercise their autonomy toward productive and valuable ends. This principle means that attempts to change children without their willing participation will probably not be effective and violate the principle of respect for persons (Drucker, 1974). There is also some evidence that a responsive environment is more effective in inducing compliance and obedience. Parpal and Maccoby (1985) have found that children are more likely to comply with adult expectations when there has been a history of adult cooperation and support of their interests and initiative.

This does not mean that we must adopt a romantic position that children should be allowed to do whatever they want. In reality, pedagogical organization makes it possible to have higher expectations, since community values are upheld throughout the community in order to achieve its goals. In bureaucratic organizations, enormous energy is expended to enforce sanctions focused on the lowest common behavioral denominator. Doing so recreates conditions that make the lowest common denominator more likely to occur. In pedagogical organizations, energy is focused on upholding community values and the creation of a satisfactory community life. Since the focus of a community's energy is on the "recreation" of opportunity and growth, there is much less interest in violating norms, even though that does occur. But where in human society does it not?

IS PEDAGOGICAL PROGRAM ORGANIZATION FEASIBLE? AN IMPLEMENTATION STRATEGY

Funding

Though lack of funds seems almost universally to be offered as the first and primary reason for the vicious cycle not being broken—"It would be great, but it couldn't be funded anyway"—we believe that it is actually the final element in the process of finding a solution rather than the immediate limitation. If we begin to think in terms of reallocation rather than new funding, however, we may find it possible to restructure the organization along the collegial lines required by professional colleagues rather than the hierarchical lines used in traditional management models to manage and direct the work of untrained people–or, increasingly in some fields, even professionals.

Utilizing the collegial model with transdisciplinary professionals (e.g., socialpedagogs) as the core staff (Barnes, 1991; Barnes & Barnes, 1996, this volume), the primary service delivery point (the residential unit) can pick up formerly dispersed functions, e.g., individual work with the children, activities as part of overall group living, casework. In a collegial model using the principles discussed, there is less friction between the system and the children, so there is less need for therapeutic intervention and supervisory control of children. Social workers can be allocated to teams for developing treatment plans, clinical consultation, and collaboration.

Table 1 is a hypothetical example comparing program budgets under the two models, in each case serving 48 children or adolescents in four units. Fringe benefits, other staff resources (psychologist, psychiatrist, nurse, etc.), and other costs (administration, food, physical plant, etc.) are not listed, since they would be approximately the same in either model.

The Transition

The collegial model quite clearly depends on there being colleagues–a team of people who share the same professional orientation, who see the demands and routines of daily life as the curriculum for learning and

TABLE 1. Cost Comparison by Model

<u>HIERARCHICAL</u>   <u>COLLEGIAL</u>

HIERARCHICAL		COLLEGIAL	

Child Care Workers
   7 per unit = 28
   @17,000[a]
	476,000	Socialpedagogs
		   7 per unit = 28
		   @28,816.75[b]
			806,869

Child Care
   Supervisors
   1 per unit = 4
   @33,440
	133,760		

ADL/Behavior Specialist	33,440		
Recreation Specialist Recreation Worker	31,200 22,269	Recreation Resource Person	25,000

Social Workers
   4 to units–Indiv.
   Counseling
   4 for Intake and
   Family Service
	262,400	Intake and Family
		   Social Workers
		   @32,800
			131,200

Clinical Director	42,000	Clinical Supervisor	38,000
Program Director	42,000	Program Director	42,000
Total	$1,043,069	Total	$1,043,069

Note: To cover the units at single coverage for 12 hours per day and double coverage for 12 hours per day requires 13,140 hours of staff time. Allowing for vacation and holidays, seven full-time staff can cover 13,349 hours, leaving a small surplus for exigencies.

[a]Salary derived from the Child Welfare League of America Salary Study (1993).

[b]This salary for socialpedagogs is made possible by the structural differences between the two models. The money saved by eliminating or changing other positions has been added to socialpedagog salaries.

cooperating, who base their work on forming relationships and therapeutic alliances and using those as the basis for conscious and strategically planned interventions. It is our belief that the lack of a professional conception of this work at the direct care level is the overriding reason for the bureaucratic controls inherent in the hierarchical model.

One way to initiate the process is to have supervisors versed in the new way of working. Their responsibility, then, is to guide and lead these untrained workers into a new understanding of the role and to help them develop the skills and perspectives required to function in a collegial model. As teams eventually evolve through positions being upgraded and workers coming in with pre-service professional education, the job of the supervisor can be redefined accordingly. Since the team will take over a number of functions that were segregated in the hierarchical model, the funds that had supported these tasks can be added to the amount available in the child care worker positions to create a pool of funds for professional direct care salaries.

CONCLUSION

We have suggested that a program organized bureaucratically is harmful to the well-being of staff and children and violates ethical norms that we would like to uphold. Organizing a program along pedagogical and human development principles is a necessity. Furthermore, it is possible, even with children and youth whose identities and abilities are damaged.

The social environment of a group care program is the result of a complex social contract between clients, staff, administration, and the community. Unfortunately, many of the poor qualities of the social environment are frequently blamed on the dysfunction of the youth and many of the good qualities are attributed to staff and program. But there is evidence to suggest that the social climate and social structure influence individual behavior (Lewin, Lippitt, & White, 1939; Ross & Nisbet, 1991). In fact, we accept this principle when it applies to the social environment from which our children and youth come; it is time that we accept responsibility for the contribution of the social climate in our programs to the maintenance and creation of dysfunctional behavior and identities in the children we serve.

REFERENCES

Barnes, F.H. (1991). From warehouse to greenhouse: play, work and the routines of daily living in groups as the core of milieu treatment. In J. Beker & Z. Eisikovits (Eds.), *Knowledge utilization in residential child and youth care practice* (pp. 123-155). Washington, DC: Child Welfare League of America.

Barnes, F.H., & Barnes, L. (1996). The convergence of the Israeli and the European experience: Implications for group care services in the United States. *Residential Treatment for Children & Youth, 13*(3), 49-62.

Child Welfare League of America. (1993). *Salary study.* Washington, DC: Author.

Drucker, P. (1974). *Management: tasks, responsibilities, practices.* New York: Harper and Row.

Goffman, E. (1961). *Asylums.* Garden City, NY: Doubleday.

Hardy, L. (1991). *The fabric of this world.* Grand Rapids, MI: Eerdmanns.

Johnson, D.W., & Johnson, R.T. (1989). *Cooperation and competition: Theory and research.* Edina, MN: Interaction Book Company.

Kipnis, D. (1976). *The powerholders.* Chicago: University of Chicago Press.

Kipnis, D. (1984). Technology, power and control. *Research in the Sociology of Organizations, 3,* 125-156.

Kipnis, D. (1987). Psychology and behavioral technology. *American Psychologist, 42*(1), 30-36.

Levy, Z. (1993). *Negotiating positive identity in a group care community: Reclaiming uprooted youth.* New York: The Haworth Press, Inc. (Also published as *Child & Youth Services*, 1993, *16*(2).)

Levy, Z. (1996). Conceptual foundations of developmentally oriented residential education: A holistic framework for group care that works. *Residential Treatment for Children & Youth, 13*(3), 69-83.

Lewin, K., Lippitt, R., & White, R.K. (1939). Patterns of aggressive behavior in experimentally created "social climates." *Journal of Social Psychology, 10,* 271-299.

Maccoby, E.E. (1992). The role of parents in the socialization of children: An historical overview. *Developmental Psychology, 28*(6), 1006-1017.

MacIntyre, A. (1984). *After virtue: A study in moral theory.* Notre Dame, IN: University of Notre Dame Press.

Parpal, M., & Maccoby, E.E. (1985). Maternal responsiveness and subsequent child compliance. *Child Development, 56,* 1326-1334.

Rosenhan, D.L. (1973). On being sane in insane places. *Science, 179,* 250-258.

Ross, L., & Nisbet, R.E. (1991). *The person and the situation: Perspectives of social psychology.* Philadelphia: Temple University Press.

Steinberg, L., Elmer, J.D., & Mounts, N.S. (1989). Authoritative parenting, psychosocial maturity, and academic success among adolescents. *Child Development, 60,* 1424-1436.

Stuck, E.N. (1994). Comment as a panelist on group care. Annual Conference of the Association for the Advancement of Social Work with Groups, Hartford, October 1994.

Thomas, G. (1994). *Travels in the trench between child welfare theory and practice.* New York: The Haworth Press, Inc. (Also published as *Child & Youth Services*, 1994, *17*(1/2).)

White, D. (March 6, 1995). [Interview on Fresh Air Radio]. Washington, DC: National Public Radio.

The Role of National Youth Policy in the Development of Residential Education in the United States

Heidi Goldsmith
Andrew B. Hahn

SUMMARY. The role of the federal government in youth policy in general, and residential education policy in particular, has been limited to targeted programs that have been subject to change and instability, with the exception of the large scale, publicly funded Job Corps program. State and local governments have been considered to be the most appropriate governmental units to develop and implement residential policies. Services have tended to be fragmentary and vary widely in quality. Residential treatment programs have received the broadest financial support, whereas developmentally oriented residential education programs are still very isolated, and it is not likely that the federal government will have a strong presence in supporting them. But the government can play an important role in facilitating information exchange about the best practices, providing for

Heidi Goldsmith, who was co-organizer of the residential education study seminar in Israel, is affiliated with the International Center for Residential Education, Suite 109, 3726 Connecticut Avenue NW, Washington, DC 20008. Andrew Hahn is affiliated with the Heller Graduate School for Advanced Studies in Social Welfare, Brandeis University, Waltham, MA 02254-9110. The authors wish to acknowledge the assistance of Debbie Fink and Yael Eran. Some of the material on national youth policy presented here is drawn from Hahn (1993).

[Haworth co-indexing entry note]: "The Role of National Youth Policy in the Development of Residential Education in the United States." Goldsmith, Heidi, and Andrew B. Hahn. Co-published simultaneously in *Residential Treatment for Children & Youth* (The Haworth Press, Inc.) Vol. 13, No. 3, 1996, pp. 99-115; and: *Residential Education as an Option for At-Risk Youth* (ed: Jerome Beker and Douglas Magnuson) The Haworth Press, Inc., 1996, pp. 99-115. Single or multiple copies of this article are available from The Haworth Document Delivery Service [1-800-342-9678, 9:00 a.m. - 5:00 p.m. (EST)].

99

technical assistance, helping with networking, and supporting basic research about residential education, most of which is operated through the private sector. *[Article copies available from The Haworth Document Delivery Service: 1-800-342-9678.]*

This article describes American youth policy and what is an extremely modest part of national policy, support of residential education options for disadvantaged youth. The article begins with a discussion of national youth policy, its origins and intellectual traditions. We develop the theme that the federal role in support of residential education, or for that matter, nearly any other kind of youth policy, has been modest historically and is likely to remain so for the foreseeable future. Historical as well as contemporary examples of national youth policy in support of residential education are presented, along with descriptions of some residential education models today. The article concludes with a recommendation for policy makers to concentrate on building the capacity of the emerging residential education field through special studies and other knowledge development activities and on assisting providers of residential education in both the public and private sectors. While such a proposal is modest, it is entirely in keeping with the limited nature of the federal involvement in youth policies.

Why explore the national youth policy landscape? The principal reason is to better understand the possibilities for growth in residential education. For example, it costs approximately $6,000 per year to support a young person from a household receiving AFDC, $12,000 a child in foster care, and perhaps $40,000 for congregate care. Even the most ardent supporters of residential education have indicated that residential education is costly. How likely is it that the federal government will step in as an active partner in the development of a new system of residential education?

Certainly at the rhetorical level, there have been countless stories in 1994-1995 about the "end of the family" and the need to "reinvent the orphanage." Daily newspaper stories, television talk shows, and screenings of the classic movie, *Boys Town*, have focused the imagination of the American people on new forms of residential education for young people who cannot or should not be cared for by their families.

Is this just another American sound bite made louder by national elections or is America prepared to explore the role of the national government as a partner in the development of the residential education field? By exploring some key themes in the general field of youth policy, as well as the specific field of residential education, we can begin to address these questions.

LIMITATIONS ON THE GROWTH
OF A TRUE NATIONAL YOUTH POLICY

Even with large historical swings in national youth policy, there has been a remarkable consistency in the ideology and organizational shape of the national government's approach to its young people. The consistency is reflected in five major ways and gives pause to anyone who predicts that the federal government's role in residential education will become expansive:

1. A consistent belief is that much of youth policy (for example, education, employment, and training) are private matters, best left to individuals, their families, and the marketplace. It follows, then, that the organization of youth policy has not actively intervened with the private side of youth issues, namely families and the labor market. "Supply-side" policies focused on changing "deficient" young people have dominated the youth development field. Youth policy has not spent much time considering environments of any kind; residential education in particular, again with the exception of the Job Corps, has not figured prominently in national youth policy debates;

2. An associated belief, as we will show below, is that the national government should step in only when unusual circumstances dictate its presence. This involvement is then seen as transitory, rather than as part of the permanent public policy landscape. Empowered by the notion that youth policy should be dynamic and responsive, national administrations, every four years, have felt free to alter the system. Serious consideration has not developed in support of any kind of permanent youth policy, whether residential or otherwise;

3. Most youth programs have, from the outset of the modern era, been add-ons and adjustments to a delivery system originally created for adults, sometimes with inappropriate results. For example, today's employment and training system–the Job Training Partnership Act–serves young people only as part of the adult legislation. There is no separate youth development legislation in the United States other than the symbolic Young Americans Act of 1989, an Act that was passed without an appropriation;

4. Fragmentation of responsibility at the federal level has been a cornerstone of federal youth policy throughout the modern era of youth programming and policy. A recent review by one of the authors documents 188 federal programs for youth spread over six federal agencies with little coordination or consistency among them (Hahn, 1995). Thus, the "system" of policies serving young people in the

United States might be better characterized as a galaxy of planetary systems, each having its unique history, policy debates, linkages with other systems, and record of performance. Residential education, like all youth development strategies, is spread across these various domains; and

5. Generally, youth programs have been locally managed, and, to the extent that there have been federal funds, this has rarely been an exclusive source of project funding. Nevertheless, much of the intellectual direction in national youth policy has come from activities supported by the federal government, especially support of program research and development. As the following section will show, even in the New Deal era, the Federal government deferred to the states and local governments for assistance aimed at the subset of the needy who were thought to be persistently poor.

A BRIEF HISTORY OF AMERICAN YOUTH POLICY

The modern era of youth policy has its roots in the New Deal, following the most dramatic market failure of this century, if not in the history of our country–the Great Depression, when unemployment rose to almost 25 percent. The federal government responded with massive public works and income support programs that bolstered the economic security of a large number of American families. But it is important to consider that the New Deal programs that were put into place as a result of the Great Depression primarily helped the mainstream working population of young adults and middle-age people (and their children) rather than "target groups" of youth populations per se.

Some New Deal residential programs were authorized to allow young men and women to live in camps where they were engaged in public works programs. These camps were not educational communities. They were seen as only temporary necessities. Documentaries and oral histories reveal vividly that the camps did a poor job of providing a safe and secure environment for young children of jobless participants. The involvement of the policy makers of that period in the residential field was anything but a planful approach to "youth development."

Equally important, the federal government placed responsibility during the New Deal for the chronically dependent population (what we would call today highly "at-risk" or "welfare" families) with the states and local governments. The National Conference on Social Welfare (1985) cites the Committee responsible for drafting the Social Security legislation of the New Deal era: "With the Federal Government carrying so much of the burden for pure unemployment, the State and local government we believe should resume responsibility for relief . . . " (p. 64).

Anticipating the current debate about state block grants for welfare reform, the New Deal established the principle that the federal policy role should be episodic, temporary, and limited to responding to national emergencies, such as unpredictable swings in macroeconomic conditions. Frances Perkins, Franklin D. Roosevelt's Labor Secretary, said in 1935 that "Federal grants-in-aid are a new departure," but she regarded them as a necessity in the short-run because many states were having difficulty helping their poorest citizens. With the subsequent growth of social welfare spending in all sectors, it is sometimes forgotten that this was the original mind-set of policy makers.

Federal youth policy mirrors these developments; sadly, it was never designed to be a proactive strategy to develop the capacities of young Americans. Since the New Deal, the federal government has stepped in to assist states and individuals with problems that it hoped would improve after a limited period of federal involvement. Accordingly, national youth policy has a built-in brake that has evolved over the decades since the New Deal: every time youth problems have led to federal involvement, the national government has felt pressure to target youth services on young people most in need as the primary method for allocating inadequate resources. This decision has invariably led to an erosion of broad-based public support for the new national programs, triggering the long-standing belief that the poorest populations are best served by local and state-based programs. Even today, the federal role in public elementary and secondary education is only 8 percent of total spending on public schooling.

The expansion of social welfare programs that occurred during the Great Society/Nixon era of the 1960s and early 1970s marks the start of the modern era of federally funded youth policies and programs. This expansionary period (1961-1973) was typified by a strong federal role, and the development of diverse and broadly based programs for various populations. This era was followed predictably by a decade that might be characterized as an attempt to consolidate and decentralize the diverse federal programs developed in the 1960s. The most recent period (the 1990s) may be characterized as one marked by a significant cutback in federal funding, a return to state strategies through block grants, and a general reexamination of the federal role.

The centerpiece of the War on Poverty launched by President Lyndon Johnson in 1964 was the Economic Opportunity Act, which established (among other things) several education and job training programs for youth. The first of these, the Job Corps, provided comprehensive services–

remedial education, literacy, occupational skills training, job placement, health care, life skills, and counseling–to low-income, disadvantaged youth aged 16 to 24 in a residential setting for up to two years. The Job Corps, of course, has endured through the present day. There are now 110 Job Corps centers operating across the country, and they serve 63,000 low-income youth per year. The Job Corps is currently again the subject of debate in the Congress amidst allegations that Job Corps centers are unsafe environments and that the program is too expensive. (More on Job Corps and its costs is presented below.)

A second of these programs, the Neighborhood Youth Corps (NYC), provided subsidized community jobs for low-income youth. This subsidized jobs strategy for youth later flourished under the Comprehensive Employment and Training Act (CETA) in the late 1970s but was greatly curtailed under the national legislation that replaced CETA, the Jobs Training Partnership Act (JTPA) in the 1980s. The NYC experimented with a summer jobs component which today has become the largest federal youth program, the Summer Training and Youth Employment Program. It serves between 600,000 and 700,000 poor youth through short-term summer jobs, with about a third of the youth also receiving minimal basic education services. National funding for this program is also under review as this article is written. In federal youth policy, nothing seems to be sacred or permanent.

Where did responsibility and accountability lie during the expansionary periods of youth programming? The 1960s generated many diverse, new initiatives aimed primarily at helping disadvantaged youth overcome difficulties. Responsibility and administration of the various programs were, from the outset, scattered among various federal agencies. For example, the Office of Equal Opportunity had been given responsibility for the Job Corps, Headstart, and the Community Action Program. The Department of Labor had responsibility for the Neighborhood Youth Corps and other federal employment programs. The then Department of Health, Education and Welfare had responsibility for the various educational initiatives. Among the major challenges today is making coordinated strategies work at the federal, state, and sub-state levels–this task originates in the piecemeal approach bequeathed to us by early youth policy planners.

State government in particular mirrors the fragmentation of youth policy at the federal level; states rarely have the resources to confront the challenge of establishing a developmental approach to youth policy and programs. At the local level, on the other hand, there are many interesting community approaches to fostering a true youth-serving system. In these, youth program managers attempt to work closely with one another toward the goal of meeting the needs of neighborhood youth. Thus far, these promising practices have not produced a certified true success. Researchers and funders are following these developments closely, to see if these "grass-roots" approaches to youth policy are more successful than national or state-level strategies.

It might also be asked in what ways America's approach to youth policy is different from those of other developed nations. While generalizations are hazardous, it is fair to note that in at least one way, namely the connection between work and education, many other countries utilize apprenticeship schemes to do a better job than America of linking these two sectors. Sherraden (1992), in a background paper for the Carnegie Council on Early Adolescents, cites several exemplary cases of developmental and even "holistic" community-based youth services, supported by national governments around the world.

A FRAMEWORK FOR UNDERSTANDING BROAD-BASED YOUTH POLICY

Political scientists offer many analytic schemas for studying national policies. Heidenheimer, Heclo, and Adams' (1983) framework is particularly useful for the youth system. He describes a four-factor model beginning with *choices of scope*, that is, the dividing line governments choose between public and private responsibilities. In the education and training field, for example, we have chosen as our public responsibility the provision of education services to assist low income youth, but only in ways that minimize interference with labor markets or that do not threaten the sovereignty of functional families. Participation in the private economy is seen as a private choice made by young people; markets and families, in the American context, are best left alone and unfettered.

The next factor in this framework involves *choices of distribution*. This factor refers to the many questions of fairness, equity, and efficiency implicit in all policy formulations. A good example is found in America's job training system, the Jobs Training Partnership Act (JTPA) which, among other things, includes the authority for spending on the residential Job Corps program. In JTPA, targeting provisions restrict eligibility for federal training to young people from families meeting certain low income standards. How do these choices about distribution work, in terms of equity, when many poor young people above and below the income standard live in crowded neighborhoods of persistent poverty? What does it mean to target individuals and not neighborhoods? How does income testing work in school settings–the single largest provider of youth services in federal education and training–where there is a philosophical reluctance among educators to determine income eligibility? What happens when many youth are just above the "notch" of eligibility? These are all issues of distribution.

Consider the third factor, *choices of policy instruments*, which includes the instruments and tools governments choose for their policy interventions. In the United States, we rely on a complex set of relationships among federal authorities, governors, state coordinating councils, local governments, and the vendors who actually deliver the services (such as schools, community-based organizations, community colleges, private firms, etc.). We use financial set-asides, mandates, performance standards, and other policy instruments to make the partnerships work.

McDonnell and Elmore (1987) describe four general categories of policy instruments:

- *Mandates* are "rules governing the action of individuals and agencies, intended to produce compliance." There are many examples of mandates, starting with income eligibility requirements to the parameters of performance contracting regulations.
- *Inducements* are the "transfer of money to individuals or agencies in return for certain actions." Setasides and incentive funds are examples of inducements.
- *Capacity-building* instruments are the transfer of funds for the purpose of upgrading intellectual capital, human resources, and materials. The federal government's investment in technical assistance and practitioner-oriented dissemination and utilization of research are all elements of the "capacity-building" agenda.
- *System-changing* activities are the "transfer of authority among individuals and agencies to alter the system by which public goods and services are delivered." This factor lies at the heart of what policy makers try to do when they support waiver demonstrations and other initiatives hoping to get an entire system to change its approach to a problem.

The fourth factor in the Heidenheimer, Heclo, and Adams (1983) framework is *choices of restraint and innovation*. What is the balance between enforcement for compliance of rules/regulations (restraint) and innovation, experimentation, and loosening of requirements? How do such questions, for example, translate into the roles and responsibilities the federal agencies choose for themselves? How much should the federal government prescribe vs. recommend; what is the balance between the roles of cheerleader and tough cop? In the current Republican controlled Congress, a historical debate is under way about the role of federal regulation, enforcement, leadership, intrusion, etc.

Our examination of these four policy factors leads us to believe that the most appropriate and feasible policy strategy for the federal government to pursue is greater utilization of one of the policy tools described above, namely, capacity-building. For a number of reasons woven into the text below, we suggest that this modest role for the national government is the most appropriate one, given the youthfulness of the residential education field in the United States and the likely barriers to a more aggressive set of policies originating in the federal government.

A NEW VISION OF RESIDENTIAL EDUCATION IN THE UNITED STATES

The various strands in the residential education field have undergone numerous permutations over the past 350 years. Boarding schools for the elite have existed and flourished in a fairly steady manner. Psychiatric treatment centers for the emotionally disturbed and juvenile correction facilities for young "deviants" proliferated during the last century. Today, we find a mix of family preservation, foster care, congregate housing, residential training, orphanages, and even private sector youth communities dotting the residential education landscape. However, residential education for *physically and mentally able yet disadvantaged youth* (the latter, by virtue of social and economic hardship) has never played a prominent role in the history or portfolio of youth strategies in the United States. Few residential schools for these children have been started, and no clear policy or overall system of residential education for these youth currently exists.

Although residential education is not a panacea for all at-risk youth, the work of the Washington-based International Center for Residential Education and of the other authors in this volume has shown that it could and should be an option for some, particularly if residential environments are planned carefully, with a child-centered, youth development focus. The Israeli residential education system, as described elsewhere in this volume, does precisely this, and can therefore serve as a vital model for American programs.

What populations are candidates for residential education of this kind in America? Whittaker (1985) defines the goal of "institutional care" as "to provide care and treatment for children who have behavioral or emotional problems or parents unable to care for them adequately, and who require separation from their own homes and a group living experience" (p. 618). This definition would fit most children and youth presently in residential care, but there are also some who are sent (or should be sent) to residential schools because the communities in which they live are dangerous, and the local schools they would attend do not offer them the chance for a quality education, given the societal settings in which they exist. Therefore, the range of needs among the children who could (and those few who already do) benefit from residential education, as encouraged by this volume, is quite broad.

An Israeli definition of residential education, by Zvi Levy, Director of Hadassim Youth Village, views it as "a broad term used to describe education given to children who for any reason live away from 'home' in settings larger than foster families where responsibility for the children's mental support and moral guidance, usually assumed by the family, is met by professional staff" (personal communication, April 1993).

Note that this definition does not connote a "problem" within the child, but rather that the circumstances of his or her life lead to the need for the residential education option. While no one school or program can provide for the wide range of children's needs, many groups of American youth are potential candidates for participation in high quality youth communities that are organized around their developmental needs–e.g., homeless children, the marginally emotionally disturbed, those convicted of "light" juvenile crimes, those alienated from their families, those who have already been in numerous placements that did not work out, AIDS orphans, unaccompanied minors from other countries, and children from "zero-parent" families.

CURRENT RESIDENTIAL EDUCATION POLICY

There has been no shortage of residential solutions tried throughout American history to meet the needs of estranged children and youth–ranging from orphanages and almshouses, to moving out-of-home children to the clear air of the Midwest, to placing them in large child care institutions under sectarian auspices, to foster homes, group homes, adoption, and "family preservation" programs (Wolins & Piliavin, 1964).

Even with this history, there is no current explicit national policy toward group care of children, but the preferences are clear. Sentiment about the importance of the nuclear family is strong. Where government is to intervene, local government is preferred. It is assumed that the state has a right to intervene only if the parents are unable to provide adequate care or if the child violates adult laws or norms governing child behavior, and that in any case of potential state intervention in family life for alleged delinquency, young people should be protected by basic procedural guarantees. Group care of children and youth is viewed as a residual service which should be considered only when the family and established non-residential community services have failed. If group care is needed, the policy increasingly favors locally-based community residences, not large congregate institutions far from the child's home.

While there may not be a residential education "system" *per se* in the United States, there are many pieces of a system. Residential education programs are found in the federal government in the Departments of Labor, Education, HHS, HUD, and Defense, and the Bureau of Indian Affairs. With this as a backdrop, it is unlikely that the federal government itself could or should serve as the coordinating entity for improved service delivery. We believe that the federal government could, however, exercise leadership in building the capacities of the multiple fields which comprise residential education.

The Federal government's oldest and largest residential program is the Job Corps, the size and scope of which have been noted previously (pp. 103-104). At a per-student cost of over $14,000, it is an expensive program to implement but not comparatively. In Program Year 1993, for example, Job Corps served nearly 63,000 new students at an average cost per student of $14,092. The average stay in Job Corps is about 32 weeks (7.6 months); thus, the annual cost per slot is $22,371. Costs are broken down by categories: 44 percent is for training, 37 percent is for lodging and support services, and 19 percent is for administrative costs. Tetro (1995) notes that,

> For $61 a day, Job Corps offers a comprehensive program of basic medical and dental care, education, room and board, social skills development, vocational training, and job placement. This compares with Boys Town, which costs $137 per day; the Department of Defense Challenge Program, $82 per day; and the average cost of a college or university education, $77 per day according to the U.S. Department of Education.

Job Corps provides the most intense training experience of any federally funded youth initiative. A new evaluation is currently under way; the most recent previous one, done in 1982 by Mathematica Policy Research (Mallar, Keraclisky, & Thornton, 1982), established the Job Corps as an effective investment strategy for raising the post-program employment and education prospects of poor youth. Surprisingly, although millions of dollars have been spent on research and demonstration projects at the federal level, few studies exist that compare Job Corps to other residential options and that examine its recent performance. This is an example of the capacity-building role in support of residential education that we envision for the federal government.

A newcomer to the residential education field is the ChalleNGe Program, run by the National Guard, first opened in Fall 1993. ChalleNGe operates in over a dozen states. The program consists of five and a half months of residential education at a National Guard base followed by a one-year mentoring program back in the youth's community. Eligible youth must be between the ages of 16 and 18 and have dropped out of school, but they need not be low income. Information reported from the program, rather than from rigorous research studies, indicates that at least half of those entering the program graduate with a high school equivalency diploma and with much higher prospects of securing a good job than when they entered. Again, new studies would be helpful using random assignment and other appropriate research techniques.

Another federally-funded residential education program is the one for Native Americans, operated or contracted by the Bureau of Indian Affairs (BIA). There are 59 on-reservation and seven off-reservation boarding schools. Unfortunately, the Native American boarding schools have historically been used to assimilate Native Americans into the dominant white culture, and the program is therefore often viewed with skepticism by its potential clientele and many educators and youth advocates. The BIA is now developing the residential education schools into more culturally appropriate and holistic therapeutic education centers.

The wills of a few individuals have funded a small number of residential education programs. A few corporations and some religious groups have funded such programs as well. The Milton Hershey School was founded in 1909 by Milton Hershey, the founder of the well-known chocolate factory, for low-income white orphan boys. Today, it serves 1,100 disadvantaged boys and girls of all ethnic groups from all over the U.S., although the majority are from nearby Pennsylvania towns. Girard College, in inner-city Philadelphia, is another facility; it was founded in 1853 by industrialist Stephen Girard for white orphan boys. It is now coed with at least eighty percent of the student body from minority backgrounds. Girard College's target student is economically disadvantaged, with a special focus on bright motivated youth who have not been in trouble with the law. The focus at Girard is clearly educational, with the vast majority of its graduates going on to college. Funding for both the Hershey School and Girard College comes from the endowments left by their founders. The American Honda Corporation recently opened the Eagle Rock School in Eagle Rock, Colorado, but this program is too new for analysis. All of these examples demonstrate another potential role for policy makers. Here we have private schools with committed leadership. To what extent does and should the federal government draw on this expertise, document these cases, and the like?

Piney Woods Country Life School in Piney Woods, Mississippi, is a historically black boarding school founded in 1909. It, too, targets motivated low-income children, and education is its primary focus; over 98% of its graduates attend college. The four other historically black boarding schools are smaller.

A number of former orphanages have been "rescued" by sectarian or other groups and are now residential treatment centers for emotionally disabled children and youth. Boys Town, just outside of Omaha, is one of the best known residential boarding schools for emotionally disturbed and socially disadvantaged youth. It defines itself as a "treatment center" but takes its educational component very seriously (as do many other residential treatment centers). It does not have income guidelines, although the majority of the students are poor. In recent years, it switched from dorm-like living arrangements to a group home model and uses token economies as one of its primary motivating and therapeutic techniques.

MODEST PROPOSALS FOR A MODEST FEDERAL POLICY ROLE

If the future is anything like the past in youth policy, it is extremely unlikely that the federal government will ever play an aggressive role in residential education. A strong federal role in youth policy is, in and of itself, a contentious issue in policy circles. Moreover, as we have shown, residential education turns on too many sensitive and thorny issues of concern to policy makers: cost, family rights, fear of institutional settings, public imagery, and so on. We predict that new facilities will not be directly supported by federal dollars, certainly not at a scale commensurate with the nature of the social and economic problems residential education is designed to address, although the federal government is moving toward making further use of abandoned and downsized military bases and other existing resources available for residential education programs.

A more promising strategy is for policy makers to use the policy instruments and tools cited earlier in this chapter to facilitate exchanges of information, "best practices" research, technical assistance, and general "networking" among the many residential education stakeholders cited in this review. We have noted that there is little contact among many of the existing programs, no combined student recruitment program, or even simple opportunities for peer learning. Using the Heidenheimer, Heclo, and Adams (1983) framework, we recommend the exercise of a policy instrument aimed at *capacity-building*. Certainly, the residential education field needs this kind of assistance.

Capacity-building starts with definitions; in the residential education field there are rarely clear lines marking what is a correctional facility, what is a treatment center, and what is purely a residential education site. The federal government should support projects that document the variety of residential education options, establish a dictionary of terms, and so forth. There is considerable confusion in the field about the basic meaning of simple terms: to cite just one example, what is the difference between "residential education" and "residential treatment"? Many facilities with the same name (residential treatment center or group home) actually represent different settings. For example, Boys Town is termed a residential treatment center, although education is heavily emphasized and there is little one-on-one formal counseling.

A related role for the federal government, through its support of research, is the collection of basic information about participation in residential education. While we know that the main placement systems are parents or guardians, the child welfare/social service system, the juvenile justice system, clergy, school staff, and community-based organizations, we know little about who within these systems sends (or has sent) children to residential education, why, and participant characteristics.

With little research to show which programs are most effective, those referring students must rely on anecdotes and self-reported figures such as how many go on to college, how many learn a trade, how many get GEDs, etc. Maluccio (1991) contends that "the desire for sure answers to problems in child welfare has led to acceptance of programs on the basis of faith rather than realism."

The federal government and other funders should support a program of comparative studies and evaluations. There is very little research on the effectiveness of residential education. The General Accounting Office (1994) stated that:

> Residential care appears to be a viable option for some high-risk youth. However, programs seldom conduct controlled or comparison studies to determine how outcomes are linked to their treatment efforts and few programs have conducted studies to show what happened to participants more than 12 months after they left the program.

Furthermore, no consensus exists on which youth are best served by residential care rather than community-based care or how residential care should be combined with community-based care to best serve at-risk youths over time.

Another policy tool cited in our review is assistance given with the aim of changing "systems." Of course the connective tissue in all system-change projects is the personnel who work in the systems. Some attention has been devoted to the preparation of youthworkers in both residential and non-residential settings, but more research of a comparative nature would help the entire residential education system respond to new pressures. Although most adults working in the field of group residential services are committed to the children's needs, the youthwork field is often *ad hoc*, paraprofessional and, in some places, not yet officially recognized. The pay is typically low, and upward mobility is limited. Salaries and benefits depend greatly on the geographic location, auspices, and quality of programs. The federal government should focus attention on youthworker qualifications, standards, pay, and career issues.

Systems of care will not be changed without a sophisticated understanding of the cost structure that supports residential education options. This is another role for the federal government, but analyses of costs will not be easy. For instance, at the Milton Hershey School in Pennsylvania, costs per child are in the $40,000 plus range, while at Piney Woods Country Life School in Mississippi, the annual cost per child is under $20,000. Virtually all residential education programs offer high school diplomas or GEDs (based on equivalency exams) to their students, most have a tutoring program, and most have a counseling program available for those who need it, but there are large differences after these core elements are considered. Few studies or even datasets are available to compare cost structures. A hypothetical comparison of this kind is offered elsewhere in this volume (Magnuson, Barnes, & Beker, 1996).

Residential treatment centers are usually more expensive than those that focus more exclusively on education. Interestingly, however, public funding is available for residential treatment (which adopts a more medical model) but usually not for residential education. Presently, the Department of Education is against the voucher system, so funds cannot "follow the children" to the school of their choice, as proposed by many educational reformers. But it is also obvious that voucher approaches and charter schools will persist as public policy and education reforms; as these take hold, they will likely raise the prospect and profile of residential education experiments.

Note, too, that there are currently no federal plans to build public residential schools. A number of local communities are considering doing this on their own (or adapting former military bases and closed hospitals and orphanages), however, and we can envision a "system-changing" policy role for the federal government as technical assistance broker, evaluator, and facilitator.

CONCLUSION

Even with a commitment to new forms of residential education in the United States–modeled after the Israeli youth villages (as described elsewhere in this volume) or other sources of inspiration–important questions remain: Should planners seek to make their programs more community-like? Why or why not? If so, how? How should programs stimulate a positive pedagogy about culture and self-identity, as in the Israeli youth villages? What is the best way to replicate family atmospheres within the institutions, as has been done by many of the best programs here and in other countries? What of the child-centeredness of the best programs? How can residential education be tied to other efforts so as to coordinate various streams of care? How should policy makers and others help to overcome various attitudinal and image problems that have held back the growth of residential education options?

A particularly promising agenda item for policy makers is the need to firm up the linkage between universities, public interest groups, and residential education programs. We have described many questions that require further research: studies on the effectiveness of residential forms of care, information on promising approaches and exemplary practices, data on participation and success rates, networking and exchange opportunities, etc. Many university and non-profit groups are accustomed to working with policy makers and practitioners, and many have the interest and expertise to help build the knowledge base for this emerging and exciting field. The federal government and private funders should work together with these centers of knowledge development.

The residential education field is still a young and marginal policy enterprise in the United States. At the national level, it is likely to remain so. However, with limited federal resources focused on knowledge-building and the strengthening of capacity, a positive and developmentally appropriate residential education field can begin to find a toehold in the United States through local and private auspices.

REFERENCES

Hahn, A. B. (1993). National human resource policy for disadvantaged youth. In *Dilemmas in youth employment and training policy: Lessons from the youth research and technical assistance project* (Vol. 2). U.S. Department of Labor. Washington, DC: U.S. Government Printing Office.

Hahn, A. B. (1995). *America's middle child: Making age count in the development of a national youth policy*. Waltham, MA: Center for Human Resources, Heller Graduate School, Brandeis University.

Heidenheimer, A. J., Heclo, H., & Adams, C. T. (1983). *Comparative public policy: The politics of social choice in Europe and America*. New York: St. Martin's Press, Inc.

Magnuson, D., Barnes, F. H., & Beker, J. (1996). Human development imperatives in the organization of group care programs: A practical approach. *Residential Treatment for Children & Youth, 13*(3).

Mallar, C., Kerachsky, S., & Thornton, C. (1982). *Evaluation of the economic impact of the Job Corps program* (Third Follow-up Report). Princeton, NJ: Mathematica Policy Research, Inc.

Maluccio, A. (1991). The optimism of policy choices in child welfare. *American Journal of Orthopsychiatry, 61*(4), 606-609.

McDonnell, L., & Elmore. R. (1987). *Alternative policy instruments*. Santa Monica, CA: Center for Policy Research in Education. The Rand Corporation.

National Conference on Social Welfare. (1985). *Report of the Committee on Economic Security of 1935–50th Anniversary Edition*. Washington, DC: Author.

Sherraden, M. (1992). *Community-based services in international perspective*. New York: Carnegie Council on Early Adolescents, Carnegie Corporation.

Tetro, C. G. (1995, March 16). Testimony before the Sub-Committee on Post-Secondary Education, Training, and Life-long Learning, U.S. Congress, Mimeo. (Available from TDC, Inc., Bangor, Maine)

United States General Accounting Office. (1994). *Residential care: Some high-risk youth benefit, but more study needed*. Report to the Chairman, Subcommittee on Oversight of Government Management, Committee on Governmental Affairs, U.S. Senate. Washington, DC.

Whittaker, J. K. (1985). Group and institutional care: An overview. In J. Laird & A. Hartman (Eds.), *A handbook of child welfare: Context, knowledge and practice* (pp. 617-637). New York: The Free Press.

Wolins, M., & Piliavin, I. (1964). Institution or foster family: A century of debate. New York: Child Welfare League of America.

Residential Education in the United States: Some Questions, Some Suggestions, and a Look Ahead

Jerome Beker
Douglas Magnuson

SUMMARY. The authors explore some of the crucial issues on which the future success of residential group care programs for children and youth in the United States depends, including funding, legal considerations, race and culture, the role of religion, and evaluation. *[Article copies available from The Haworth Document Delivery Service: 1-800-342-9678.]*

Residential education is not a new phenomenon in the United States. It has long been the education of choice for the children of the elite, often facilitating the transmission of societal power within the same families from generation to generation (Cookson & Persell, 1985). Historically, the Black colleges have performed a similar role for many young African-Americans, not all from families in leadership roles (English, 1996, this volume). Yet much of late Twentieth Century lay and professional opinion alike has rejected residential options for meeting the needs of the growing numbers of our youth who are seen as "disattached," "uprooted," or "at risk" for various kinds of troubled and troubling lives.

Correspondence should be addressed to the authors c/o Youth Studies Program, School of Social Work, University of Minnesota, 386 McNeal Hall, 1985 Buford Avenue, St. Paul, MN 55108.

[Haworth co-indexing entry note]: "Residential Education in the United States: Some Questions, Some Suggestions, and a Look Ahead." Beker, Jerome, and Douglas Magnuson. Co-published simultaneously in *Residential Treatment for Children & Youth* (The Haworth Press, Inc.) Vol. 13, No. 3, 1996, pp. 117-124; and: *Residential Education as an Option for At-Risk Youth* (ed: Jerome Beker and Douglas Magnuson) The Haworth Press, Inc., 1996, pp. 117-124. Single or multiple copies of this article are available from The Haworth Document Delivery Service [1-800-342-9678, 9:00 a.m. - 5:00 p.m. (EST)].

117

For these young people, residential programs tend to be viewed as too costly, inevitably abusive, ineffective, subversive of family, and (partly for that reason) ideologically unacceptable (see Beker, 1991; Beker & Schwartz, 1994). Few would deny that these criticisms reflect the reality of many American group care programs today, but the frequent conclusion that they represent intrinsic defects rather than operational failures hardly seems warranted in the face of contrary examples from our own history and from other countries, as have been described in the current volume (Beker & Magnuson, 1996b). At the same time, the need for such programs increases, given rising demands for youth incarceration, growing numbers of "zero-parent" families and homeless youth (with the predictable wave of AIDS orphans not yet upon us), and overburdened, sometimes abusive, family foster care resources. For all these reasons, the exploration of residential alternatives emerges as a moral as well as a practical imperative.

Predominant residential program models in the United States tend to emphasize clinical, custodial, and correctional components. This means that their clientele tend to be viewed–and, partially as a result, to view themselves–as "sick" or "crazy," weak and dependent, and/or "bad." Good intentions notwithstanding, many of these programs appear to function so as to reinforce rather than to overcome these developmentally counterproductive images, which in turn also reinforces the negative image of the programs themselves.

Broader conceptualizations have been proposed and implemented in the United States in the past (see Beker, 1991) and have emerged in a few current and projected programs (see Miller & Caneda, 1994; Goldsmith & Hahn, 1996, this volume). Such approaches appear to have become more normative in parts of Europe (Barnes & Barnes, 1996, this volume), however, and in Israel (Beker & Magnuson, 1996a, this volume). Levy (1996, this volume) has proposed a conceptual schema that can help to close this gap by detailing a positive developmental role for group care and the components required to operationalize it.

SOME CRUCIAL ISSUES

In seeking to develop and implement constructive changes in group care programs for children and youth in the United States, whether through the application of residential education models or through other approaches, we confront a series of policy and program dilemmas that need attention if we are to be able to move ahead. Some of the most salient of these are introduced below, with brief discussion of the underlying issues they reflect.

Funding

Residential programs have come increasingly in recent decades to look for funding to the health care system (Medicaid, health insurance, etc.) and the child welfare system. Particularly with the growth of "managed care" in the health domain, however, pressures have grown for justification of expenses for residential services in terms of health deficits and medical needs. This tends to reinforce the negative definitions of residential care clients mentioned previously and to preclude reimbursement for developmentally oriented services.

Likewise, the child welfare system conditions its support on weakness and dependence rather than on rewarding the development of strengths. Although the importance of ongoing aftercare has been clearly established (e.g., Whittaker, Overstreet, Grasso, Tripodi, & Boylan, 1988), for example, such programs are typically not reimbursible and, as a result, are minimal if they exist at all. Usually, support ends at the age of 18 in any event. Thus, most current funding mechanisms tend to push the definition of residential services in exactly the wrong directions, those declaimed by their critics as noted above.

In Israel, by contrast, the enterprise–working with many of the same kinds of youth–defines the task as residential education, and it is primarily supported through the education system. Thus, the task is conceived as primarily involving learning and building rather than rescue or treatment. Commitment to clients is viewed as ongoing and permanent whether the client lives in the setting at any given time or not, even into adulthood. This does not resolve the problem presented in all human service enterprises by growing pressures for operational efficiency even at the expense of the quality of services provided, but it at least enables the program to be oriented in the desired direction. Moreover, it has been suggested (Magnuson, Barnes, & Beker, 1996, this volume), that residential education programs may be no more expensive than our traditional ones, and Levy (personal communication, March 1996) suggests reasons why they might actually cost less. More attention to this question is needed.

Legal Issues

For a variety of reasons, residential services (along with other human service programs) are frequently being shaped by legalistic rather than developmental considerations. In the face of burgeoning lawsuits, practitioners and agencies have understandably "lost their nerve," and defensive practice in many domains has become the rule. For example, it is hard to imagine how effective work with young people can proceed without appropriate touching–an arm around the shoulder or a pat on the back–yet many direct care workers are instructed not to allow themselves to act in these ways due to concerns about legal vulnerability. The legal climate in the United States makes these issues real and significant, but they are nonetheless barriers to successful services and the resulting dilemma needs to be confronted.

Race and Culture

In the United States today, we cannot talk sensibly about youth development and the establishment of identity without considering the issue of race and associated subcultural differences. In healthy families and communities, these matters are usually addressed naturally, often subliminally, in the course of daily life, but such is not the case among uprooted and disattached youth, for whom they often become more salient and underlie much disaffection and rebellion. It is these youth for whom residential alternatives will be needed; consequently, attention to racial issues is crucial.

In this context, one must question whether racially separate or mixed facilities serve best, at least in the early stages of group care placement, when identity confusion is most likely to predominate. How does each model contribute to identity development and to the eventual ability to live and work together? What components need to be different in each to avoid furthering destructive forms of separatist identities and agendas as well as the creation and reinforcement of identity confusion? Normally, one's identity comes from that of his or her family; when residential services replace the family role to a significant extent, they need to perform this function just as they need to provide food and shelter. This is an issue that may be difficult to resolve on a practical level, given legal and societal constraints, but it is one with important implications for residential services.

Religion

Religious influences have been among the few elements grounding the lives of many of our disadvantaged people, particularly members of ethnic minority groups, in the domains of identity, values, and social participation. Here again, families have been instrumental in linking young people to their cultural roots. When residential settings play the role of the family, how can such traditions and their developmental impact be maintained? In addition, since most residential programs are public and/or operate with public funding, how can the apparent conflict with our legal and cultural tradition of the separation of church and state be resolved?

Evaluation

Accountability concerns have fueled what seems to be an ever increasing search for precise, quantitative assessment of program outcomes, an expectation that is particularly acute when innovations in existing approaches are proposed. The degree of change implicit in this article and the compendium of which it is a part (Beker & Magnuson, 1996b), such as a shift from a medical to an education model, would, of course, evoke such demands. Yet few rigorous summative or formative evaluations of the effects of residential programs on the well-being of children have been carried out, and even fewer have been successful in documenting either the success or the failure of a program. It is possible that one reason for the unsatisfactory nature of these studies is that they have missed the essence of the program being assessed. Many of these studies have focused on first order and linear characteristics, such as the accumulation of skills and behaviors. If the perspectives offered in this volume have anything to offer, they may suggest that it is more important to focus on transformational qualities, second-order change (Maier, 1987).

These variables are more difficult to operationalize and to measure, but the task is not impossible. Even if we cannot touch or measure them directly, there may be indicators of their presence. It has been suggested that children and youth may be happier in the type of programs alluded to here because they more fully satisfy young people's developmental needs. Programs in the Teaching Family Model already measure (quantitatively and rigorously) the child's satisfaction with his or her progress and happiness with the quality of the program (Davis, Warfel, Maloney, Maloney, & Fixsen, 1978).

Levy (1993) has suggested that a sense of control over one's destiny is characteristic of health. It is not difficult to conceive of an instrument or an evaluation approach that would measure the child's feeling that he or she can influence the future course of his or her life as opposed to a fatalistic perspective.

Developmental theories offer another source of evaluation measures. Kegan (1982) charts changes in the evolution of meaning-making that suggest age-appropriate developmental levels that may be impacted by these types of programs. He is also critical of behavioral interventions that do not address the ends and values to which they are addressed or the interpretive framework of the child or youth.

CONCLUSION

Many readers will recognize, with differences in detail, the situation of a 12-year-old boy (this is based on a real client) living in a U.S. residential treatment setting. He has been there for three months, since his mother gave up her parental rights. Earlier in his life, he was sexually abused. He is expressing his anger and feelings of rejection, most would agree, by running away, having temper tantrums, getting into fights at school, and the usual litany of mildly deviant and rebellious acts.

Although the roots of his anger are understood by those who are working with him, he is nonetheless disruptive to others in his group and to the smooth running of the institution, and his treatment team is under pressure from the administration and direct care staff to find a solution, a way to stop his expressions of anger. There have been several meetings of the case manager, the psychologist and psychiatrist, the school counselor, the child care workers, and other agency staff. The child care staff is suspected of being incompetent by the degreed, consultative "professionals." A variety of "interventions" have been tried, but to no avail. Consideration is now being given to removing him from the program, to be placed in an even more restrictive setting.

It is likely that many of the foreign programs cited above would have much more patience with this boy. They would be less likely to create circumstances that would raise his level of hostility and defensiveness. He would be allowed more time to "cool off," to survey and adapt to his surroundings and environment before high expectations were placed on him. They would respond to him as a person, not as a collection of behaviors that need to be stopped; they would understand that the results of 12 years of rejection and abuse are not likely to be corrected in three months. Short-term compliance would be less of a concern than long-term growth.

The reason for these differences is a matter of perspective. We can learn from others the activity of thinking about how the child experiences and perceives the world. This was the lesson of the great pedagogical thinkers (Dewey, 1944; Montessori, 1989; Tolstoy, 1982), the developmental psychologists (Erikson, 1963; Piaget, 1954; Vygotsky, 1978), and modern day cognitive psychologists (Feuerstein [see Feuerstein, Klein, & Tannenbaum, 1991]; Gardner, 1991). This is also the lesson of the perspectives from Israel and from northern Europe that are presented in the volume of which this article is a part. It appears to be a lesson that this field needs to learn.

REFERENCES

Barnes, F. H., & Barnes, L. (1996). The convergence of the Israeli and European experience: Implications for group care services in the United States. *Residential Treatment for Children & Youth, 13*(3), 49-62.

Beker, J. (1991). Back to the future: Effective residential group care and treatment for children and youth and the Fritz Redl legacy. *Residential Treatment for Children & Youth, 8*(4), 51-71.

Beker, J., & Feuerstein, R. (1991a). The modifying environment and other environmental perspectives in group care: A conceptual contrast and integration. *Residential Treatment for Children & Youth, 8*(3), 21-37.

Beker, J., & Feuerstein, R. (1991b). Toward a common denominator in effective group care programming: The concept of the modifying environment. *Journal of Child and Youth Care Work, 7,* 20-34.

Beker, J., & Magnuson, D. (1996a). Residential education as an option for at-risk youth: Learning from the Israeli experience. *Residential Treatment for Children & Youth, 13*(3), 3-48.

Beker, J., & Magnuson, D. (Eds.). (1996b). Residential education as an option for at-risk youth [Special issue]. *Residential Treatment for Children & Youth, 13*(3).

Beker, J., & Schwartz, I. (1994). Does institutional care do more harm than good? In E. Gambrill & T. J. Stein (Eds.), *Controversial issues in child welfare.* Boston: Allyn and Bacon.

Cookson, P. W., Jr., & Persell, C. H. (1985). *Preparing for power: America's elite boarding schools.* New York: Basic Books.

Davis, M., Warfel, D. M., Maloney, D. M., Maloney, K. B., & Fixsen, D. L. (1978). *Consumer evaluation manual: How to assess consumer attitudes towards group homes.* Boys Town, NE: Father Flanagan's Boys' Home.

Dewey, J. (1916/1944). *Democracy and education.* New York: Macmillan.

English, R. A. (1996). Some implications of the African-American experience for the development of residential education in the United States. *Residential Treatment for Children & Youth, 13*(3), 63-67.

Erikson, E. H. (1963). *Childhood and society* (2nd ed.). New York: Norton.

Feuerstein, R., Klein, P., & Tannenbaum, A. (Eds.). (1991). *Mediated learning experience: Theoretical, psychosocial, and learning implications.* London: Freund.

Gardner, H. (1991). *The unschooled mind: How children think and how schools should teach.* New York: Basic Books.

Goldsmith, H., & Hahn, A. (1996). The role of national youth policy in the development of residential education in the United States. *Residential Treatment for Children & Youth, 13*(3), 99-115.

Kegan, R. (1982). *The evolving self: Problem and process in human development.* Cambridge, MA: Harvard University Press.

Levy, Z. (1993). *Negotiating positive identity in a group care community: Reclaiming uprooted youth.* Binghamton, NY: The Haworth Press, Inc. (Also published as *Child & Youth Services*, 1993, *16*(2).)

Levy, Z. (1996). Conceptual foundations of developmentally oriented residential education: A holistic framework for group care that works. *Residential Treatment for Children & Youth, 13*(3), 69-83.

Magnuson, D., Barnes, F. H., & Beker, J. (1996). Human development imperatives in the organization of group care programs: A practical approach. *Residential Treatment for Children & Youth, 13*(3), 85-97.

Maier, H. W. (1987). *Developmental group care of children and youth: Concepts and practice.* New York: The Haworth Press, Inc. (Also published as *Child & Youth Services,* 1987, *9*(2).)

Miller, D., & Caneda, C. (1994). *Children's Academies for Achievement: Residential academies of excellence.* Princeton, NJ: Authors.

Montessori, M. (1989). *The absorbent mind* (C.A. Claremont, Trans.), New York: Dell.

Piaget, J. (1954). *The construction of reality in the child.* New York: Basic Books.

Tolsoy, L. (1982). *Tolstoy on education: Tolstoy's educational writings 1861-62* (Selected and edited by Alan Pinch and Michael Armstrong; translated by Alan Pinch), East Brunswick, NJ: Associated.

VanderVen, K. (in press). Point and level systems: Another way to fail children and youth. *Child and Youth Care Forum.*

Vygotsky, L. S. (1978). *Mind in society: The development of higher psychological processes* (Michael Cole, Ed.), Cambridge: Harvard University Press.

Whittaker, J. K., Overstreet, E. J., Grasso, A., Tripodi, T., & Boylan, F. (1988). Multiple indicators of success in residential treatment. *American Journal of Orthopsychiatry, 58*(1), 143-147.

Index

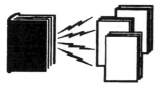 Haworth
DOCUMENT DELIVERY
SERVICE

This valuable service provides a single-article order form for any article from a Haworth journal.

- *Time Saving:* No running around from library to library to find a specific article.
- *Cost Effective:* All costs are kept down to a minimum.
- *Fast Delivery:* Choose from several options, including same-day FAX.
- *No Copyright Hassles:* You will be supplied by the original publisher.
- *Easy Payment:* Choose from several easy payment methods.

Open Accounts Welcome for ...
- Library Interlibrary Loan Departments
- Library Network/Consortia Wishing to Provide Single-Article Services
- Indexing/Abstracting Services with Single Article Provision Services
- Document Provision Brokers and Freelance Information Service Providers

---

MAIL or *FAX* THIS ENTIRE ORDER FORM TO:

Haworth Document Delivery Service
The Haworth Press, Inc.
10 Alice Street
Binghamton, NY 13904-1580

or FAX: 1-800-895-0582
or CALL: 1-800-342-9678
9am-5pm EST

PLEASE SEND ME PHOTOCOPIES OF THE FOLLOWING SINGLE ARTICLES:
1) Journal Title: _____
    Vol/Issue/Year:_____Starting & Ending Pages:_____
    Article Title:_____
    _____

2) Journal Title: _____
    Vol/Issue/Year:_____Starting & Ending Pages:_____
    Article Title:_____
    _____

3) Journal Title: _____
    Vol/Issue/Year:_____Starting & Ending Pages:_____
    Article Title:_____
    _____

4) Journal Title: _____
    Vol/Issue/Year:_____Starting & Ending Pages:_____
    Article Title:_____
    _____

(See other side for Costs and Payment Information)

COSTS: Please figure your cost to order quality copies of an article.

1. Set-up charge per article: $8.00
   ($8.00 × number of separate articles)   _____

2. Photocopying charge for each article:

   1-10 pages: $1.00   _____

   11-19 pages: $3.00   _____

   20-29 pages: $5.00   _____

   30+ pages: $2.00/10 pages   _____

3. Flexicover (optional): $2.00/article   _____

4. Postage & Handling: US: $1.00 for the first article/
   $.50 each additional article   _____

   Federal Express: $25.00   _____

   Outside US: $2.00 for first article/
   $.50 each additional article   _____

5. Same-day FAX service: $.35 per page   _____

   GRAND TOTAL: _____

METHOD OF PAYMENT: (please check one)

❑ Check enclosed   ❑ Please ship and bill. PO # _____
   (sorry we can ship and bill to bookstores only! All others must pre-pay)

❑ Charge to my credit card: ❑ Visa;   ❑ MasterCard;   ❑ Discover;
   ❑ American Express;

Account Number: _____   Expiration date: _____

Signature: ✗ _____

Name: _____   Institution: _____

Address: _____

_____

City: _____   State: _____ Zip: _____

Phone Number: _____   FAX Number: _____

MAIL or *FAX* THIS ENTIRE ORDER FORM TO:

Haworth Document Delivery Service   **or FAX:** 1-800-895-0582
The Haworth Press, Inc.   **or CALL:** 1-800-342-9678
10 Alice Street   9am-5pm EST)
Binghamton, NY 13904-1580